MY WAR – VIETNAM

1968~69 / 1971~73

An Autobiography

Short Stories about What I Did and
What I Saw While Serving with
Special Forces

Author

Albert Kittredge

<u>MY WAR – VIETNAM 1968~69 / 1971~73</u>

DEDICATED

To all who served in that ill fated war.

Table of Contents

Introduction

I'm a Vietnam Vet who until recently, like so many other veterans of that ill-fated war, did not talk a lot about what I saw and did. That changed a few years ago when I realized if we don't talk soon all that history will be lost. I recently celebrated my 81st birthday so time's a wasting.

I wasn't a hero but I did serve alongside many heroes. Every Vietnam Vet could and should write their story – depending on where we were and in what timeframe, everyone's story would be different. I take pride in not embellishing my stories – what you read or hear from me actually took place.

Chapter 1

A Special Tribute to the Fallen:

PFC Dallas Padgett was the only American killed under my command in the two and one half years I served in Vietnam. I was in Special Forces (Green Beret) and we were always short medics so Dallas was on loan to us from MACV. He was a good medic and we treated him as a member of the team. He pulled his share of patrols and was killed in an ambush while we were working with the US Navy Swift Boats. I remember writing the dreaded letter to his parents. We made him an "Honorary Green Beret" and sent a green beret along with all the patches with the letter. I corresponded with his mother a couple times after that because like all parents she wanted details on his death. We named the camp dispensary after Dallas. His profile can be seen at

http://www.virtualwall.org/dp/PadgettDL01a.htm

SSG Perry Browning was the senior medic at one of my SF camps. He was on a patrol a month after I was transferred to another camp. His patrol got in a serious firefight where several Vietnamese soldiers were wounded. While caring for the wounded a Viet Cong lobbed a grenade into the makeshift aid station. Perry bent to scoop it up but it went off before he could throw it back killing him instantly. I sometimes look at some of the SF Vietnam era message boards and saw where Perry's family was asking if anyone knew him. I connected with his wife and sent her several photos I had of Perry which she shared with his now grown children. Perry's profile can be seen at

http://www.virtualwall.org/db/BrowningP N01a.htm

CPT Louis Geneseo was my replacement at A-414 which was the last SF camp I commanded during my initial tour. He and the B team commander **LTC Marty Beck** were killed in a helicopter crash 10 days after I turned over the camp to CPT Geneseo. Ten days earlier and I would have been on that helicopter. I corresponded with his wife a couple times as she was trying to find out what happened. Profiles of both CPT Geneseo and LTC Beck can be seen at http://www.virtualwall.org/dg/GeneseoLJ01a.htm

http://www.virtualwall.org/db/BeckMR02a.htm

I could go on with seven more names. Although I know the circumstances of their death I did not know them that well - I did however place two of them on a helicopter for the first leg of their final ride home. To each of them I say "God Bless You and Rest in Peace. I hope your families were able to carry on after your passing".

Chapter 2

Riding to War in a Huey

"Back in the day" the army was cranking out lots of pilots. I applied but it didn't take long for them to figure out that I was partially color blind. Those of you who have taken the test have seen the little book with lots of various colored circles arranged in such as fashion that a normal eye sees a number. You had to correctly see the number in the majority of 20 odd flip pages – well I could only guess 3-4 and it was a wild guess at that. I'm from New England and always wondered why folks went ga-ga every fall when the leaves changed to vibrant colors – I just never thought it was much of a big deal. Now I realize I wasn't seeing the true colors. OK, I could not be a pilot so I became a Green Beret instead.

Helicopters came of age in Vietnam. They replaced the horse of the cavalry, the truck for moving personnel or supplies and the ambulance for the medical folks. Of course they also gave commanders and senior staff a platform to insert themselves in the action from a safe distance.

Just about everyone who served in Vietnam had numerous rides in helicopters either moving from one safe place to another or for the folks out in the bush, moving from a relatively safe base camp to a not so safe place trying to make contact and annihilate the Viet Cong. Once I was assigned to an A-team I spent a lot of time in helicopters doing just that. So much so, that I started keeping track of the number of times I flew from our SF base camp to an area where we hoped to engage the enemy – 25 of these airmobile assaults and you were qualified for the Air Medal. Once I had documented my 25 insertions I stopped counting, figuring you could only wear one ribbon. In hindsight I should have kept counting because subsequent awards would have included an oak leaf cluster. I likely could have added 2 or more oak leaf clusters because we did a lot of airmobile assaults.

Here are a few of my "Riding to War in a Huey" stories:

The best seat on a Huey:

During most of the Vietnam era Huey's set up for combat insertions were void of interior seats or doors. The normal load was 4 crew members (Pilot, Copilot, Crew Chief and Door Gunner (The crew chief also acted as door gunner on one side while in flight) and 9 combat loaded Americans or 12 combat loaded CIDG (aka "little people") We stuffed 6 CIDG into the middle and three sitting on each side in the open doors with their feet dangling out into space just above the skid. We always sent 2 American SF (USSF) with each such operation and were usually accompanied by 2 of our Vietnamese counterpart SF (VNSF) team members. I broke it up so that our 2 USSF did not ride on the same chopper. I always thought the center spot sitting in the open door was asking for trouble because there was no place to hold on to other then your fellow soldier on your left and right. I never saw anyone fall out but it just never felt safe to me. The guys on the left and right of this threesome sitting in the open door could hold on to the side of the aircraft. If we were going into what was thought to be a cold landing zone (LZ) I liked to sit on the side behind the pilot so we could communicate by shouting or hand signals. If it was a hot LZ I liked to sit next to the stanchion separating us from the door gunner to make sure he stopped firing and had raised his gun before we jumped off. We joked in a gallows humor fashion that the most dangerous man in Vietnam was a door gunner because nothing will ruin your day faster than a door gunner firing as you jump to the ground and the chopper takes off – the forward movement of the chopper puts the wildly firing door gun right at your back.

The time I nearly drowned:

I spent a short time at the intermediate level headquarters as a staff officer while waiting for spot to open up out in the field. I was eventually assigned as an A-Team Leader of a Special Forces (SF) camp and started riding to war in a UH-1D Huey. I'm not sure how other teams did it but at the two camps where I was the A-Team Leader we all took turns going outside the wire. That was not always the case at one of my camps which is why I replaced the guy originally assigned there. The only times I or the Team Sergeant pulled ourselves off the "outside the wire roster" was just before the end of the month when we had to compile the monthly report for higher headquarters. Our mission included having at least one company size unit out all the time. If we were not careful (you might say cunning) they would go just over the horizon, set up for two days with very little patrolling and come back saying they did not see a thing. I found that if I could get helicopter support, a good way to insure we covered our sector, was to insert them at least two days march away from camp. Some patrols were just a slow walk back to camp but at least we were covering our sector.

One time during the monsoon season when most of the terrain was covered with water I was on the 2nd lift of a company size unit being inserted into the far end of our sector. By the time I arrived at the landing zone at least half the unit was already on the ground sloshing around in ankle deep water. I stepped off the skid of the Huey expecting to do the same but to my surprise dropped into a bomb crater. The water was over my head and I was weighed down by a pack, boots, full web gear to include a couple hundred rounds of ammo and weapon. I would have drowned if two CIDG soldiers had not seen my plight and laughingly pulled me soaking wet out of the hole. I wonder what ever happened to those two soldiers and if they are alive today – I expect not.

I think we can get you all on:

One occasion I had responded with a relief force to assist a unit which had been ambushed and badly mauled. We got things sorted out, medevac'd our wounded and settled in for the night. The next morning only half the number of choppers needed to carry us back to base camp were available so we had to return piecemeal with a 30 minute turn around per flight of 4 aircraft. I put the mauled unit along with their dead on the first flight. I waited with the relief force but there were too many of us to all make it on the next two flights.

One of the pilots who had been there when we were inserted the night before told me to add one "little people" to each load. We still ended up with too many. The lead pilot and I discussed the wisdom of leaving myself and a handful of CIDG on the ground in a known "hot area" while we waited for another lift. He said "What the hell, it's flat here with no trees and the humidity is about right, hop in, I think we can get you all on".
Remember – 12 "little people" was the normal max load. I'm only 150 pounds soaking wet so I could be counted as one

of the "little people" - we piled 16 on that chopper - add the crew for a total of 20. The engine strained and shuddered. The skids would lift a few inches off the ground but then set back down. More straining of the engine and we lifted about a foot but still not above the grass. Finally the pilot thrust the tail in the air and started forward with the front of the skids parting the tall grass. After what seemed like an eternity of whipping through the grass we picked up enough speed for the pilot to "pull pitch" and we shot up into the air.

Chapter 3

FAC's, Bird Dog's & Other Flying Machines

Sharks and more sharks:

I first arrived "in-country" in the Spring of 1968. There was a few days lag between being reassigned from the replacement center at Long Bien to 5th SFG(A) in Nha Trang. I used that time to reconnect with my old 1st Sergeant who was now the Sergeant Major of a nearby helicopter unit. One thing led to another and I was invited to accompany one of the unit "work choppers" as it made it's twice weekly run with mail and resupplies to outposts on the islands just off the coast in the South China Sea. If my memory serves me right there was no manifest, no recording of who was on the flight or anything like that. Just a handshake with the crewmembers and off we went. The scenery was right out of a tourism magazine and you'd never know there was a war going on until you got close to an outpost with its sandbags and mortar pits. At some of our stops I caused somewhat of a stir when I, as a young Green Beret Captain stepped off the bird – you could see the question in some eyes "What the heck is he doing here?" The thing I really remember is how clear the South China Sea was and all the huge sharks that just seemed to be waiting for someone to develop engine problems and ditch into the water.

USAF FAC's, Agent Orange & Free Fire Zones:

I was initially assigned as the Personnel Officer (S-1) of B-41 located in the Vietnamese City of Moc Hoa. We were at the top of the Mekong Delta in IV Corp. This was an interim assignment while I waited for an A-Team to open up. Our compound was the only US military compound in Moc Hoa. In addition to the B team element which supported 5-6 A teams spread out along the Vietnam / Cambodia border we hosted an Army/Air Force airfield control element, and a USAF Forward Air Controller (FAC) who initially flew a single prop Cessna O-1 that was later changed to a front and rear prop Sky Master O-2A.

I became friends with the Air Force FAC who was on his 2nd tour, the first having been as a high speed bomber pilot. He was now using his knowledge to locate targets and bring in close air support. He knew I was bored with my desk job so often invited me to accompany him as he patrolled the Free Fire Zone (FFZ) that had been set up all along the Vietnam / Cambodian border. The FFZ was set up by moving all the locals a couple miles off the boarder and declaring that anyone found in the FFZ would be considered hostile and dealt with accordingly. Of course some of that land was originally someone's home, farm land or fishing hole. It was not unusual to have them sneak back from time to time. Our CIDG were locals themselves so tried to sort it out but often times to their own peril, i.e. "Be quick, tell me are you local rice farmer or VC. Tell truth or I shoot and call airstrike on you".

I read recently that a Free Fire Zone would be considered a war crime in today's politically correct environment.

During the three months I was the B-41 S-1 I logged a lot of hours with my FAC buddy. A few incidents still come to mind.

We flew off to the side while waves of C-123 aircraft rigged as spay planes sprayed defoliant (Agent Orange) on the forested areas. Later on when I was assigned to an A-Team we went into some of those areas and it resembled the face of the moon – dark and dusty, without a living thing growing.

We also stood well off from the target area and observed when V's of B-52 bombers laid what was called an Arc Light on suspected VC staging areas. The concussion waves from the explosions could be felt in our small

16

aircraft even though we were way off to one side.

One time I looked down to see a sampan being pulled up into the reeds. By the time we got back around just the tail end was visible and it eventually disappeared. Rice farmer, fisherman, or VC? We couldn't tell, but they were in a Free Fire Zone and obviously didn't want to be seen. We called in two fast movers and marked the target area with white phosphorus rockets and watched as one jet dropped high explosive bombs and the other napalm. Times have changed because the use of napalm is now considered a war crime.

Shortly after turning in the Cessna 0-1 and getting checked out on the twin engine O-2A (one engine in front and one in rear) my hot-shot FAC friend cut the front engine as we were taking off from the Moc Hoa airstrip - scared the hell out of me. The air plane shuddered just a few feet above the ground but eventually gained enough airspeed to lift us above the town at the end of the runway. Young and dumb and having the time of our lives – if anything bad happened we figured it would happen the other guy.

US Army 0-1 Bird Dogs:

In addition to the Air Force FAC we also hosted a one plane surveillance unit that basically flew the Free Fire Zone collecting intelligence and serving as the B-41 commanders personal aircraft. Our B-41 Commander, LTC H. also served as the Province Senior Advisor – which is probably why we rated our own 0-1 airplane, aka "Bird Dog". Some of our A-Teams had small airstrips so I frequently commandeered the 0-1 to visit the teams, deliver mail and at the end of the month, deliver a huge sum of Vietnamese money to pay the CIDG.

One team did not have an airstrip so if a Huey was not available we'd fly the 0-1 low and slow over the camp while I dropped a mail sack containing mail and thousands of dollars out the door.

Yep, we did that back then.

We almost crashed:

One time while riding the backseat of the O-1 we observed a native thatch hooch out in the middle of the Free Fire Zone. It appeared to be deserted but this was a Free Fire Zone so we decided to shoot it up. The pilot would make a low and slow pass off the side of the hooch while I leaned out the window with my M-16 on full automatic – I had several magazines of ammo loaded just for these situations - one ball, one tracer and one ball. We had made two or three passes when all of a sudden the aircraft jerked, went up and down and sideways. At the same time the pilot was clawing at the back of his neck and howling something awful. What had happened was a piece hot brass from my M-16 rifle had gone down the inside of his flight coveralls. It is a wonder we didn't crash – I'm sure the casualty report would have been written to make us heroes brought down by enemy gun fire. I wrote a couple reports similar to that, complete with awards and all, while I was the B-41 Personnel Officer (S-1).

Soon after the hot shell casing incident our Bird Dog pilot decided he needed a more efficient firepower system. He scrounged some rocket pods and two M-60 machine guns which he and his crew fabricated under each wing of the aircraft. The machine guns triggers were pulled by jury rigged wire treaded through a series of eyes ending with a handle hanging in the cockpit. He now had a fully functioning low tech attack plane. I flew with him one time while he was working out the kinks in the trigger system. We made a run on a suspected VC hidey hole when the wire triggering system jammed and the gun would not stop firing until it ran out the entire belt of ammunition.

Like I said before - young and dumb and having the time of our lives.

Geeeezzz, did you see that?

During my 2nd tour (71-73) our involvement in the war was winding down. Many American units had left and more were leaving every month. For the most part the US Army was reduced to an advisory, training and logistics role. I knew a guy who had been aide to the general officer now overseeing the training mission – he sent his former boss a copy of my orders and I soon had a letter signed by the general saying that I was to "by pass go" and be assigned directly to the FANK Training Command (FTC). For those not familiar, FANK stands for Forces Armees Nationales Khmeres – Cambodian Army. About 10 days after arriving "in-country" I was the assigned as the Operations Officer (S-3) of Phuoc Tuy Training Battalion (PTTB), located on the Long Hi peninsula. This was just across the bay from Vung Tau and about 50 miles by road from Saigon. PTTB had just recently moved from Chi Lang and was in the process of retrofitting an old ARVN NCO Academy which had been stripped clean of all electrical and plumbing when the ARVN moved out. A Seabee unit came to our rescue and after about a month we no longer had to operate on generators or smell burning crap every morning.

Once we were up and running we started training Cambodians who arrived in battalion size units. They arrived with their own leadership but nothing more than the clothes on their back.. After issuing uniforms, web gear and individual weapons everyone went through basic training. After basic we put them through advanced individual training (AIT). Most remained infantrymen but during the AIT phase some were trained as machine gunners, mortar men, medics or radio operators. The officers were given leadership training.

Near the end of the AIT cycle they conducted field training in an area known to be "relatively" secure. That does not mean it was entirely secure. It appeared there was an uneasy truce and if we didn't mess with the local VC they wouldn't mess with us. That was not always the case. There was one memorable occasion where a FANK unit and their USSF trainers got too close to what appeared to be an abandoned VC village. A sniper shot one of the trainees. The return fire from the friendly's used up about all the ammunition the Cambodians had. Their US cadre called for a resupply but by the time we were able to get a helicopter to our landing pad it was well past dark. We loaded several cases of M-16 and M-79 ammo into the chopper. I jumped aboard, plugged my pilfered headset into the radio/intercom system and away we went. We flew to the general vicinity of our troops but had a difficult time locating them. As we circled the area the door gunner exclaimed "Geeeezzz, did you see that?", as a fire hose of tracers arched out of the darkness toward our direction. Yeah, we all saw it!! We quickly located our troops, dropped down to offload the ammo resupply, and loaded up the wounded Cambodian. We then "**di-di mau**" the hell out of there.

Don't look now but we just lost an engine:

While the Cambodian training program was being phased out, those of us left in-country was busy providing refresher training to the Army of Vietnam (ARVN). I was on two Mobile Training Teams (MTT) doing just that but when I extended at the end of my normal one year tour was assigned to the old FANK Training Command (FTC) headquarters in Bien Hoa as the Operations Officer (S-3). In addition to managing the drawdown of the FANK program I was up to my eyeballs filling ARVN requests for MTT's. One time the FTC Commander, COL H. and I were catching a ride back to Bien Hoa on a C-130 after visiting one of our MTT's in Da Nang. About half way into the 3-4 hour flight the flight engineer said "Don't look now but we just lost an engine". We looked and sure enough the right outboard engine propeller was not turning. The flight engineer went on to explain there was nothing to worry about because the C-130 could fly with only 2 of 4 engines and could even make an emergency landing on 1 engine. Well that was comforting news but COL H. and I were both relieved when we safely landed back at Bien Hoa.

Chapter 4

Shot at and Missed

This took place in the spring of 1969 soon after I was transferred from my first SF camp Tuyen Nhon (A-415) where the LLDB (VNSF) commander and I were not seeing eye to eye because I suspected him of skimming the payroll and holding back on bonuses due the CIDG when they scored a big cache of weapons and munitions. The B-41 commander LTC H. used that as a pretense to move me to Thanh Tri (A-414) where there was a lack of emphasis on going outside the wire.

I said this before in my other short stories – I'm not sure how other teams handled the "outside the wire" operations but at both of my camps we all took turns. Anything larger than a platoon operation included at least one American - all company size operations had two. The only time the Team Sergeant or I pulled ourselves from the rotation was at the end of the month when we had to write up the monthly activities report. Even then, if it looked like contact with the enemy was eminent I jumped to the head of the line. The following story was one such case.

Thanh Tri was located in what was called "the finger" area right up against the border of South Vietnam and Cambodia. It received that nickname because on the map it appeared as if someone clichéd their fist and pointed a finger. We even made up a plaque which showed our distain for the enemy who at the time took advantage of the sanctuary they enjoyed in Cambodia.

We were on the western perimeter of B-41's area of responsibility but often conducted joint operations with the SF camp to our west – 50 years later my memory is a little vague but I believe that camp was known as Cai Cai. This incident took place when we were inserted as a company size unit via helicopter as a blocking force while the adjacent camp pushed the VC/NVA back toward the Cambodian border.

This was a joint operation which meant folks on the ground had lots of supervision from headquarters types flying in relative safety overhead. I say relative safety because just the month prior our B-41 commander, LTC H. had the Huey he was riding in sit down in what was thought to be a safe area to pick up an American wounded and set off a booby trap which punctured his lung. He almost died before they stabilized him enough to be medevac'd stateside. He was replaced by LTC B. who along with his VNSF counterpart, and the B-41 Operations Officer (S-3) CPT B. were running the show.

My Forward Air Control (FAC) buddy from a previous story was flying overhead in his 0-2A just in case he was needed - well he was needed.

We were just getting set up when our forward element was attacked from the rear flank by a force that realized what we were doing and came at us from across the border.

GAME ON – if they could attack from across the border we would do our best to make sure they didn't make it back to their safe zone in one piece.

It took awhile but the FAC located a trio of fighter/bombers who at my request laid down a carpet of high explosives and napalm right along the river/canal that separated Vietnam from Cambodia. That took care of the direct assault on our flank but we continued to receive fire from across the border.

SFC M. the USSF who was with me on this operation called that one of our CIDG had been wounded. He was bringing him back to the hastily set up Command Post (CP) just inside a tree line where the VNSF commander and I were located. Once the wounded man was evacuated to our location I sent SFC

M. back to the flank to make sure we were ready in case the VC/NVA came across the border again. At the same time I called for a medevac to land just to our rear for the wounded CIDG soldier. One of our CP group popped smoke at the designated landing zone (LZ)

The medevac was inbound so I threw the wounded Vietnamese CIDG soldier over my shoulder and made my way to the LZ with my radio operator in tow. As I entered the open area all hell broke loose with a machine gun going rat-tat-tat and the dirt kicking up around my feet just like you see in the movies – in fact that was my immediate thought along with "GD that guy is shooting at me". I'd been shot at before, but truth be told, I'd been in the area of lots of gunfire before but this was the first time I was sure the shooter was actually looking at me.

By this time the medevac chopper was about to go into hover mode. Thankfully my radio operator was right behind me so I was able to contact someone in the command chopper who was watching this whole thing unfold. We were able to get the medevac chopper called off before we had more than one wounded on the ground. I still had the wounded CIDG draped over my shoulder and carried him back several hundred yards to a relatively safe area where the medevac returned and rushed him to a medical hospital. (As a foot note to this story he recovered and returned to our camp and his family several weeks later)

A short parley between the headquarters staff flying above and us folks on the ground, resulted in a decision that because of the rules of engagement about not going into Cambodia that we had better call it a day before we created an international incident.

The helicopters which had inserted us earlier were on standby back at the airfield just down the street from B-41 Headquarters in Moc Hoa – they were called and we were soon on our way back to camp.

This was a fairly significant engagement and everyone back at camp had been glued to the radio. When SFC M. and I returned the first thing we did was go into the team house and have a cold beer – actually several cold beers. Everyone gathered around to hear our story. I remember not being able to stop talking – Being shot at and missed is a high that few people ever experience.

Within the next few days I wrote up a valor award for SFC M. – Unbeknown to me someone from the B-41 staff also put me in for the same award which I received on my way out of country as I was passing through 5th Group Headquarters in Nha Trang.

That was nice but what I am really proud of is the words that LTC B. put on my OER which said "I have personally observed CPT Kittredge engaged in battle. He is a fierce fighter and great combat leader." Well yeah – that is why LTC H. transferred me to Thanh Tri!

Unfortunately a few days after signing my OER, LTC B. and my replacement CPT G. were KIA when the helicopter they were riding in was blown out of the sky as it hovered low to investigate a suspicious object on the ground.

Chapter 5

Huh, What'ya say?

The Mike Force which was billeted just across the airstrip from B-41 in Moc Hoa hosted a contingent of airboats which were used during the monsoon season. They were great once the rivers and canals flooded out of their banks for responding to reports of a possible infiltration through the Free Fire Zone (FFZ). These FFZ were created by moving all civilians approximately 2 miles off the border between South Vietnam and Cambodia. Anyone seen in the FFZ was considered hostile and subject to appropriate action. Prior to creation of the FFZ many people farmed or fished the area and were not too happy to be forced from their homes – some defied the government and returned.

Our US Air Force Forward Air Controller (FAC) or in the case of Moc Hoa, our own US Army Birddog assigned there because the B-41 Commander was also the Province Senior Advisor (PSA), flew the FFZ and reported any suspicious activity. During the monsoon season airboats were a good way to check out what was going on before calling in a more lethal response.

My first experience with airboats came when the senior advisor to the airboat contingent, SFC F. needed a second American to accompany him on a planned sweep of the left sector of the FFZ. At the time I was the S-1 of B-41 and was tired of pushing paper so quickly volunteered.

Before I get into the details I'll try to paint a picture of a military airboat based on memory of 50 plus years. They were made of fiberglass and could travel at a rapid clip on very little water – in fact they would go for a short distance on little more than the dew on the grass.

My guess is they were 16-18 feet long and 4-5 feet wide with an upswept curve from rear to front. A powerful engine drove an aircraft style propeller in the rear of the vessel. Right behind the propeller was a couple of venetian blind style shutters that were controlled by the driver with a "joy stick" to steer the airboat. Most recon airboats were manned by a crew of three. The driver and the boat commander sat side by side just to the front of the engine. The boat commander had a PRC-25 hooked up to a set of earphones to talk with the overall operation chief in one of the other airboats. The 3rd crew member was a gunner standing up front manning an M-60 machine gun set on a pedestal. The boat commander and his crew communicated over the roar of the engine with arm and hand signals.

On this, my first airboat operation, we were making a general sweep through the FFZ when we came upon a couple of hooches which should not have been there - remember, anything other than friendly military in a FFZ was presumed to be hostile.

I am not sure how it came about but we ended up circling the two hooches like a band of Indians in a western movie and firing them up with our M-60 machine guns. When it was over we went in and found an old mamsan lying dead in a fresh pool of blood. Definitely not our finest hour.

Not long after that I was assigned as the team leader of A-415 (Tuyen Nhon). I remained there about 3 months before being transferred to A-414 (Thanh Tri) where I found a platoon of airboats attached to our camp for the duration of the monsoon season. We used them to patrol the FFZ which extended all along the Vietnam / Cambodian border. The CIDG liked them because they were a quick way to check out intelligence without having to slosh through water or paddling our own sampans to the suspicious activity. They were fun and exciting to work with but did have several drawbacks;

At the beginning or end of the monsoon season you had to be careful or you would "run a ground." This often happened when you were tooling along at high speed and encountered a dike in a flooded rice paddy. Sometimes you just shot over it much the same as a car hitting a speed bump but if the dike was a wide one you'd end up grounded.

We only had 6-8 airboats and not all were working at the same time so if we did run into much more than the occasional farmer, fisherman or smuggler we were often outnumbered and had to rely on hit and run tactics until reinforcements could be called in.

The roar of the engine announced our presence for at least a mile in all directions. We countered that by speed which did not give anyone much time to react before we were on them. This was fine when there was lots of water but at the beginning or end of the monsoon season we often found ourselves channelized which allowed the enemy to evade or worse yet set up an ambush along the route we were forced to take.

The roar of the engine also reduced communications between crew members to shouts or arm and hand signs. Communications between boats and higher headquarters, i.e. back to camp was done via headsets hooked to PRC-25's but it was also very difficult. The roar of the engine setting right behind your head was so loud that we often joked that the only way we would know if someone was shooting at us was when the guy beside us fell over dead.

We could always tell who had been on a recent airboat operation because when you'd talk with them their response was "Huh, What'ya say?

Chapter 6

The Souvenir VC Flag

Don't ask me how the logistics folks came up with it but folks at the Special Forces A and B team level were on their own for chow or rations. The US Army absolved themselves of responsibility for our rations by giving us the sum of $30 per month in what was officially called "Rations Non Available or RNA – try to subsist on the local economy on the princely sum of $30 per month. The B teams could make do by collecting the $30 from each team member along with the same from others billeted in the compound such as Forward Air Controllers, Intelligence teams and various logistics folks. Even then it took creative manipulation by the team member assigned to oversee the unit mess. At the A-team level there was no way $360 was going to feed 12 men 3 square meals a day for a month. Not to fear – we made out and here is how it went at the two teams I had the honor of leading during the 1968-69 timeframe. I suspect other teams did something similar.

All of the SF camps in the B-41 area of responsibility were pretty well established by the time I arrived in 1968. Each had been built by Seabees or US Army engineers. Most had an inner and outer perimeter with the USSF teams inside the inner perimeter. The team house was the focal point of team life. At both of my camps the team house contained the radio room, sleeping quarters for about half the team, a latrine / shower, kitchen and open area for eating and a makeshift bar.

I am not sure how it was at other camps but the ones where I was the team leader we broke up the sleeping arrangement so the same skill sets were not quartered in the same room or building. Team members not quartered in the team house slept in nearby adjacent buildings according to their additional duties. For example, one of the weapons men slept in the building where a makeshift weapons repair shop was set up and extra weapons were stored. The team member assigned the extra duty of keeping track of cots, blankets; spare this, spare that, had an alcove off the supply room. They might share their room with one of the radiomen or medic. If space allowed everyone had an individual room or in a couple cases a large room with a divider down the middle. The team leader, team sergeant and team XO were not all billeted in the same building. In both of my camps I slept two rooms down from the radio room. Unless on patrol, assigned to the FOB or as was often the case with our medics who might have an overnight patient in the dispensary, the entire USSF team slept within the inner perimeter.

Most of the time we kept one of our 14 man team members (12 man SF team augmented by 2 man civil affairs team) off site on an administrative or logistics mission which was combined with a visit to the PX, some in-country R&R and scrounging for chow and other goodies. Some guys were better at it than others but everyone was expected to come back with stuff to make team life easier.

When someone was sent off on one of these logistics missions they might depart with cash and a shopping list from individual team members. For sure the team sergeant presented them shopping list along with the cash to replenish the team beer and soda bar.

How this worked was each A- team in our area had one or more refrigerators located in the common area of the team house filled with beer and soda. These beverages were purchased in bulk through the PX system in Can Tho or any other location where there was a large enough number of US troops to warrant a PX. At the time, if you bought at least a pallet (80 cases) you could get it for 10 cents a can. If you explained your situation to whoever was in charge of the warehouse you could usually mix and match in order to come up with a full pallet. We'd purchase it in bulk at 10 cents a can and sell it back to ourselves at 25 cents a can. We'd keep track of consumption on the honor system using a grease pencil board taped to the side of the refrigerator. If you were a visitor to the team you were expected to deposit the correct amount in a coffee can. The team sergeant kept the books and collected at the end of each month. The profit was used to pay a cook, cook's helper and one or more house keepers and laundry girls.

Ok, now that we have the beer and soda covered and of course Green Berets have the reputation of consuming more than their share of the former, but we still needed to put some food on the table. If we wanted to go native, and we did for a few items, we'd tell mamsan what we had in mind, give her a few piaster's and she'd buy things off the local market to provide an excellent meal. What about pancakes, meat and potatoes, canned goods, milk, etc and all the fixings? Remember, we only got $30 per man and even at 1968-69 prices that wasn't going to buy much.

However, a skilled NCO with the appropriate story and tear in his eye, along with a few captured VC weapons could do wonders if he visited the logistic centers responsible for providing food and other consumables to regular American units. The folks in charge of these consumables didn't seem to have a problem with accountability and were often willing to share if they received something in return. Some food came dehydrated, canned or in powder form but if you followed the instructions it would make a pretty good meal. A "big score" was honest to goodness ice cream but you'd better not get it out of the donor's freezer until you were sure you had an aircraft and some block ice to carry it directly back to camp. Many a gallon of ice cream turned to soup on the tarmac or PSP runway when transportation fell through.

Most SF camps had a supply of captured weapons and gear that could be bartered to rear echelon logistics folks. We had a ready supply of these items because we paid the CIDG troops a bounty for captured weapons, ammunition, mines and explosives. The only caveat was that each item had to be verified by an American before pay out. This requirement kept them honest but it also created some scary situations if they came across a trip wired grenade or booby trap with no American around. It was not unusual for them to come back to camp to collect 50 cents for a grenade with only the wire or fish line wrapped around it to keep it from going off.

The trophy that was guaranteed to get us a couple cases of steaks or a helicopter ride back to camp with the ice cream still frozen was a captured VC flag. We had plenty of captured weapons but I don't recall that we ever captured a VC flag. Have no fear; the SF mind can be cunning and creative at times. One of our housekeepers had a sewing machine and was good with needle and thread so we had her sew up a few flags. We then sent the cook to the village to purchase a couple live chickens to add to her soup. Chicken blood was dabbled on the flags as they were rolled on the ground. Add a few bullet holes and you had a genuine VC flag captured in a fierce battle. All you needed now was a good storyteller and a gullible rear echelon logistics guy looking for a souvenir.

I've often wondered how many of these "genuine" VC flags now hang on the walls of the local VFW or American Legion.

Chapter 7

Get This GD Truck Moving!

As an incentive to the CIDG we paid a bounty for captured enemy weapons, explosives and ammunition. There was a sliding scale with the greatest value placed on automatic weapons, factory produced mines, high explosive ammunition, grenades, homemade booby traps and individual rounds of ammunition. Everything had value to the unit or individual who found it and had it confirmed by an American.

Weapons, ammunition and stable explosives were usually brought back to camp for inventory and documentation. Weapons were often kept as souvenirs by the USSF or VNSF team members. Some of the weapons were traded with rear echelon folks (often referred to as REMF) for chow or other items to make life back at camp more bearable. Ammunition and explosives were inventoried and destroyed.

Things got hairy when a unit without an American present encountered a homemade booby trap. The unit or individual who found it was hell-bent on collecting the 50 cents for such a find. They'd painstakingly unarm the booby trap, or often an entire series of booby traps – wrap the tripwire or string around it and carry it in their back pack for days until they got back to camp and proudly dumped their find at the feet of an American who could validate and pay the bounty.

While I was at Tuyen Nhon (A-415) in late 1968 early 1969 we had several American units use our airstrip as a temporary launching point for operations.

Because we were living there and they were just passing through they always asked us to accompany them.

This worked out fairly well because they had the helicopters, fire support and other logistics that we could only dream about. One event that pissed me off was when one unit called me on the radio and asked for a platoon of "mine detectors" to accompany them the following day. I didn't consider our CIDG as "mine detectors" and told the unit S-3 that I expected his troops to share responsibility of taking "the point" if we were to continue to work with them. Another thing that I noticed when there was an American unit in the area was signs of Marijuana and other drug use. I never saw it at the two camps I had the honor of leading unless there was an American unit nearby.

On one joint CIDG / American forces operation we discovered a major arms and ammunitions cache the VC had buried with the intention of coming back later. This was the "mother lode" of all arms caches during my time in Vietnam. It included shoulder fired weapons, tank mines, anti-personnel mines, mortar rounds, recoilless rifle rounds and thousands of small arms ammunition. There was so much that it took a C-47 helicopter to bring it back to camp for inventory.

Here is a sample of what we found....

(top to bottom down the center) torpedo for clearing minefields or fencing; small anti-vehicle/tank round; large anti-tank round; rifle propelled grenade, large mortar round; potato masher style hand thrown grenade; small mortar round; large anti-tank mine; (left side) box of electrical detonators; can of detonators; B-40 shoulder fired rocket round; (right side) AK 47 ammunition; 12.7mm machine gun ammunition.

The CIDG unit which found it was ecstatic because they had visions of boo-coo bounty $$ running through their head. Once we had it all inventoried it amounted to over $4000 in US dollars which converted to several thousand VN piaster's.

This payout was the straw that broke the camels back in my relationship with the VNSF commander. We didn't have a great relationship right from the beginning because he never went "outside the wire" – in fact none of the older team members remembered him ever going on operation.

Once it became obvious there was to be a big payout for the recovered VC weapons and ammunition the VNSF commander decided it would go to him and that he would use it to throw a party for the entire camp. We had a party but it was certainly not a $4000 party. We also never saw any other improvements in the life or living conditions for the CIDG soldier or their families. We came damn close to drawing down on each other over that. A couple months later there was a command issue at another camp and I was transferred there.

Once everything was inventoried it became our responsibility to destroy it so that it did not return to use by the enemy or get back into the hands of the CIDG who were not above turning something in twice for a double bounty. That task fell to the USSF Combat Engineer.

Tuyen Nhon (A-415) had a short road network going to the airstrip, down through the CIDG dependent village and on to the hamlet of Tuyen Nhon. In better times the road would have gone to Moc Hoa and beyond but all the bridges had been destroyed earlier in the war.

Because we had that short road and an airstrip we rated a ¾ ton truck. I think every A-team had some sort of wheel vehicle transportation – most of it was sling loaded into camp by CH-47 due to lack of functioning highways. Two years later when I returned to Vietnam as part of the Cambodian (FANK) training program and the US units were going home we had lots of vehicles – some on the books, some given to us without supporting paperwork by a departing US unit and some procured the SF way – Ummmm, maybe that could be the topic of another short story.

Half our team was off site for R&R, chow run or accompanying the CIDG on operations so I volunteered to help our SF engineer and a handful of CIDG take the captured munitions a safe distance outside the wire to destroy it.

This was a big cache which required several sorties by the ¾ ton truck.

Our engineer assured me he had done this before so I just followed his lead. We piled it in one big pile with the small arms ammo on the bottom followed by grenades, then the anti-tank mines and booby traps. We interlaced blocks of C-3 connected together with primers and detonating cord (det-cord) over the top of the ammunition. The final addition to this demo-man's brew was a fuse lighter and short length of timer fuse, double primed at the det-cord end going to the blocks of C-3. In hindsight we had too much for one blow but what did I know?

After double checking all connections we hollered "fire in the hole", pulled the pin on the fuse lighter and everyone hopped in the ¾ which was sitting there idling pointed to the berm of an old fighting position just outside the camp perimeter.

The USSF engineer sergeant was at the wheel. When he floored the accelerator the ¾ lurched forward, coughed and died. As you can imagine the pucker factor which was already high shot up from an excited scale of 10 to a frantic scale of 1000. Our two CIDG helpers abandoned the vehicle and started running like hell toward the berm.

All I remember saying was "Get this GD vehicle moving". After a couple feeble attempts the ¾ finally started and we barreled full speed toward the fleeing CIDG. We all arrived at the old abandoned fighting position at about the same time and came to a screeching halt. Just as we ducked behind the berm that gigantic pile of enemy munitions went skyward. It rained metal fragments for what seemed a long, long time. When all was quiet we went back to check and there was a hole several feet deep and twice as wide. Young and dumb and on the adventure of a life time.

Chapter 8

"Druggie" or just trying to stay alive?

"Back in the day" SF medics, especially out on the A-teams, were as close to being doctors as you could get without actually going to school and placing MD after their name. They and a few CIDG soldiers whom they personally trained as assistants took care of the daily medical needs of a battalion sized unit of indigenous soldiers and their dependent families.

They could stabilize life threatening battlefield wounds until the victim could be flown to a medical hospital to be seen by a real doctor. Minor ailments, scrapes and bruises were no problem.

Delivery of babies and aftercare, although not an everyday occurrence, were still fairly routine. At Tuyen Nhon (A-415) we had a baby born with a very pronounced harelip – our team medics, SSG Perry Browning and PFC Dallas Padgett, made arrangements to have the baby and it's mother flown to the Philippines where the birth defect was corrected – this made a very positive impression on the CIDG dependent village when they returned.

Unfortunately both USSF medics were KIA before their tour was up. PFC Padgett was killed during my watch – SSG Browning was killed shortly after I was transferred to another SF camp.

Every SF camp dispensary had copious amounts of medications, many of which today would be considered controlled substances. By copious amounts I mean gallon jars of pills after pills. If there was a system of control I was not aware of it. There were a few pills that every SF soldier carried in small amounts in his kit bag.

No one liked the infamous malaria pill but it was a standard item of issue by the team medic every Monday. He would stand there and watch you gulp it down. If you were offsite on operation, R&R, chow run or wherever, you were still supposed to take your malaria pill. No one liked the malaria pill because it's effectiveness was still unproven. It also gave you a serious case of diarrhea. Just imagine being on R&R with a self-inflicted cased of diarrhea.

To counter the diarrhea we had a tiny pill named Lomotil. You had to be careful when using Lomotil because if you took too much it would really stop you up.

In a hot, wet and dirty war zone even scratches and bruises could turn into serious infections. To counter that we all carried a 10 day supply of tetracycline, a broad based antibiotic good for most anything if you caught it before the offending germ or bacteria had a chance to really settle in. We've learned later in life that overuse can screw up your immune system but didn't know any better at the time.

The two pills that got a lot of use were barbiturates and amphetamines, commonly referred to as "reds and greens". We used these to induce much needed sleep or to stay wide awake depending on the situation. I suppose some folks abused them but I did not see any of that at either of the camps where I was the SF team leader. I personally used the "greens" or amphetamines to stay awake at night if we set up an ambush along a well known infiltration trail or canal. I seldom used the "reds" or barbiturates because whenever I did, I'd wake up groggy with a bad taste in my mouth.

One occasion I am glad I had popped a "green" to stay awake when we set up an ambush along the Bo-Bo Canal. The Bo-Bo Canal originated deep inside Cambodia and was a well traveled infiltration route. At the time Cambodia was "off limits" to US Forces, therefore was used as a sanctuary and staging area by the VC and NVA.

The Bo-Bo was on the far edge of the A-415 Area of Responsibly (AOR). It also formed the boundary line between IV Corps and III Corps. I accompanied a platoon size unit to set up an ambush based on recent intelligence. We motored well up the canal in fiberglass Boston Whaler style boats powered by 20hp outboards.

We disembarked about a mile from the Vietnamese / Cambodian border and set up a hasty perimeter for an early evening meal then proceeded by foot to a preselected ambush site further up the canal. We moved into position just before dark and settled in to see what came up or down the canal. I popped a "green weenie" to make sure I stayed awake.

The boats minus the troops were sent back to camp. All of this boat traffic passed along the small canal and CIDG family village running beside our camp, out past the hamlet of Tuyen Nhon into the Van Ca Dong River and up into the Bo-Bo Canal on the opposite side. We rationalized that none of this boat traffic was highly unusual because we often motored up the canal to launch sweeps along the border. We'd then sweep west and end with the troops bending south and coming out opposite the SF camp where they were ferried across the small canal by sampan or motorized boat.

Midnight came and went with nothing happening - soon it was past 0200. I was about to pop another pill to keep from nodding off when we heard the wommp, wommp, wommp of helicopters heading our way from the III Corps side of the canal. In less time than it takes to write this, there was a giant search light slowly going up one side of the canal and down the other. I didn't need another pill because I was now wide awake. We immediately recognized what was going on and the old pucker factor was really kicking in.

Either by coincidence or perhaps they were reacting to the same intelligence – we were set up in the same area that was being patrolled by a "firefly team". They consisted of a Huey with a giant searchlight backed up by 2 Cobra gunships flying a few hundred feet higher just waiting for the Huey to light up a sampan or any enemy personnel along the Bo-Bo at 0200 hours in a Free Fire Zone. No doubt about it if they saw us we were in deep do-do.

Without any movement on our part, my VNSF counterpart and I, along with the help of our very scared but able interpreter conveyed to the CIDG the importance of not moving a muscle. They were told not to look up or move any weapons or anything shiny that might catch the reflection of the searchlight. In the meantime I was on the horn (radio) back to camp who patched me through to our B team in Moc Hoa. We attempted to contact someone from III Corps who might know the radio frequency of the unit flying overhead. All this time the searchlight would go down one side of the canal to the point where we thought it would move on and then cross over and slowly come up the opposite side. This went on for some time – we never did make contact with the helicopters and they never did see us. They eventually lumbered off toward the interior of III Corps. No one needed pills to remain awake until daybreak. We were thrilled that we were still there to see the sun come up.

We called for the Boston Whalers to pick us up for the ride back to camp. Once there I submitted a quick after action report, popped a couple "reds" and was soon in a deep sleep.

Chapter 9

Trip Wire Watch Repair

I've got to set the stage for this story by going back to my enlisted time in the 101st Airborne at Ft Campbell, KY – this was back when the 101st was Airborne and not Airmobile. I left school (quit) at the end of the 10th grade and joined the Army on my 17th birthday in 1956. After basic I was assigned directly to Ft Campbell where the 101st was being reactivated after being disbanded soon after WWII. The 101st set up it's own jump school – my 1st five jumps were on Yamoto DZ out of C-119's.

After pinning on our wings, our entire jump class was assigned to the 506th Airborne Infantry Battle Group. Fifty of us went to E Company. That's right, Easy Company, 506th Infantry of the "Band of Brothers" fame – little did any of us know it at the time. All of our NCO's and most of our officers were WWII or Korea Vets.

The 506th ran an Advanced Individual Training (AIT) program and we were soon Currahee paratroopers (We Stand Alone – Together).

In spite of being a snot-nosed smart ass, I was also a pretty good soldier and was soon assigned to the company communications section as the company commander's radio operator. Back in those days it was the backpacked PRC-10 and the jeep mounted GRC-8. During parachute operations I jumped right in front of or right behind the company commander, all 150 pounds of me doing the duck waddle with a Griswold Bag containing all my gear plus that confounded PRC-10 and extra battery. Maybe that is what prompted me to go to OCS so I could have someone else carry the radio.

Being the company commander's radio operator didn't get me off the duty roster so I pulled my share of KP and guard duty. At Guard Mount the sharpest trooper was selected as the supernumerary. Eight out of ten times I was selected and didn't have to walk a post unless someone became sick or there was an emergency. However the following day you had to go to group headquarters to be the group commanders personal orderly – with a little bit of luck he'd let you off at noontime.

In late September 1958 the 1st Sergeant sent me to compete for the soldier of the month award. I made it and was selected as the 506th Airborne Infantry Battle Group Soldier of the Month for October 1958. (I still have the newspaper clipping to prove it). At the time, Major General Westmorland was the commander of the 101st - he came down and presented me with a nice watch in front of all the troops.

Ok, fast forward time – There was no war going on so I was discharged in 1959 but almost immediately joined the Vermont Army National Guard. They must have seen something in me because after being promoted to sergeant they offered me the opportunity to attend OCS. Our involvement in Vietnam was ramping up so soon after obtaining a commission I volunteered to come back on active duty – they needed cannon fodder so they took me.

My first assignment was to Ft Carson where I thought as a new 1LT I'd be a company XO or staff officer – how naïve of me. When I reported in to

Squadron Headquarters the commander said "We've been waiting for you - get your ass down to C Troop, you're the new troop commander". A year later I volunteered for SF, went to a year of Vietnamese language school and on to the adventure of a lifetime. I took my lucky General Westmoreland watch with me.

About halfway through my initial Vietnam tour I was transferred from Tuyen Nhon (A-415) to Thanh Tri (A-414) in a small shake up of the leadership by the Moc Hoa (B-41) commander, LTC H. His instruction to me was to get more aggressive than was currently going on at that camp or he would find someone who could. I don't believe it was a coincidence that the VNSF commander was replaced at the same time.

The new VNSF commander Dia-uy Diem and I were of the same mindset and got along fine. Neither of us was reluctant to go "outside the wire". We always kept at least a company size unit out all the time. One of my favorite tactics was to secure helicopters to carry them to one of the far edges of our area which was at least a two day walk back to camp –

longer if you did it in zig-zags. That kept them from just walking out of sight of camp, setting up a defensive perimeter and coming back two days later saying they didn't see a thing. I accompanied one such insertion along with the VNSF XO. My trusty General Westmorland watch was now carried in my pocket because I'd broken the watchband and lost one of the little pins that held the band in place.

The first day and evening were uneventful as we made a zig-zag along the Vietnam/Cambodian border. Around mid-afternoon on the second day we were making our way toward the general direction of camp spread out in a modified column of threes. I was with the command group in the center. There was a loud boom about 30 yards to my left and the 2nd man in that staggered column was thrown skyward. We were all seasoned soldiers and froze in place because we knew in a nanosecond that he had triggered a mine or booby trap. The 64 dollar question was – were there anymore and if so where?

We all looked to our right, left, front and rear and it did not take long for shouts coming in that we were indeed in the middle of a fairly large booby trapped area. I looked to my immediate front and saw a thin wire stretched less than two steps away – if not for the unfortunate CIDG soldier to my left it would have been me going skyward.

A closer look revealed the wire led to a beer can size grenade hidden in a clump of grass. One of the CIDG who was much more experienced at these things than I, carefully undid the wire and wrapped it around the grenade. Others to our left and right were doing the same thing with booby traps they had discovered. Some of the CIDG were smiling because every disarmed booby trap was worth 50 piaster's in bounty money. We had a policy that bounties were paid if an American personally verified the item.

While the troops were clearing the booby trapped area I called for a medevac chopper. One of the CIDG whom we had trained as a medic administered 1st aid to the wounded soldier whose legs and crotch area were badly mangled and bleeding profusely. We moved him well to the rear of the booby trap area so that the medevac would not trigger any mines or booby traps we may have missed.

Once the wounded man was on his way to the nearest hospital the troops brought all the disarmed booby traps to me for counting and verification. If I'd not been there they'd have gingerly placed all the booby traps in a rucksack and one soldier would have been tasked to carry it until they returned to camp for verification.

I wonder if that unlucky CIDG soldier did much praying as he carried his unstable load back to camp.

I retrieved the trip wire from the one that had been directly in my path as a souvenir. We then placed all of them in a shallow pit, placed a block of C-3 explosive on top and blew them to smithereens.

The remainder of the walk back to camp was uneventful. A couple days later our USSF civil affairs officer, who doubled as the team funds officer, paid the CIDG company commander the equivalent of about $20 for the recovered and destroyed booby traps.

I found that the trip wire I retrieved as a souvenir fit perfectly in the holes on my General Westmorland watch – I still have that trip wire repaired watch.

Did I Just Kill 9 Innocent People?

I'm going to jump forward on my story telling to a time during my 2nd tour (1971-73). I'm doing this so that folks who have been reading my previous short stories don't get the impression that it was all fun and games.

At the start of my 2nd tour I was the Operations Officer (S-3) of the Phuoc Tuy Training Battalion (PTTB) with the mission of training battalion size units of Cambodians and sending them back into the fight in their own country. We brought them in by the planeload, outfitted them with clothing, web gear and weapons.

They were then given a modified version of basic and advanced training which took 16-20 weeks before being shipped back to Cambodia with all their new gear and a double load of ammunition.

We were located on the Long Hai peninsula not far from Vung Tau which before the American drawdown hosted several US units and served as an in-country R&R Center.

Vung Tau also had an Air America section which was collecting up helicopters deemed too old for economical return to the USA with their units that were being rotated home as part of the USA drawdown. (For my non-SF readers, Air America was part of the CIA contribution to the war). This particular Air American section was overhauling "slicks" and gunships for eventual transfer to the ARVN or Cambodians. The section contained several former combat pilots who were bored testing refurbished aircraft and eventually ferrying them to their new owners.

With the drawdown our helicopter support at Phuoc Tuy was limited to a "work chopper" one day a week which we had to share with Long Hai, a sister camp with the same Cambodian training mission just up the road. There was always a struggle between the two camps as to who would get the chopper first and for how long – no one ended up completely satisfied.

Once I learned about the Air America unit in Vung Tau I paid the operations section a visit and explained our situation. Before I left they had agreed to fly over to see our camp and perhaps work out ways of support while at the same time keeping their pilots happy with flight time. I also drove away with a snub nose .38, holster and several boxes of ammunition – amazing what you can get if you're nice to people and have a good story.

Within the week the Air America operations officer and his boss flew over and landed at our one helicopter size landing pad just across the road from the perimeter that surrounded the old AVAN leadership academy which had been stripped of all wiring and plumbing before being turned over to what was renamed PTTB when a third of the Cambodian training mission was moved from Chi Lang in early summer 1971.

After a briefing, tour of our facility and observation of training in progress, they agreed to support us in the event of an emergency and also in routine flights whenever our schedules were mutually agreeable. We looked at this as a win-win for everyone. We got the support and their pilots got some flight time which was not centered around check rides or delivery flights to new owners.

After working this routine for awhile and knowing that some of the helicopters were being converted to gunships complete with mini-guns and rocket pods, and prior to being turned over to the Cambodians, I got the idea of putting on a demonstration of how a unit in contact with the enemy could call in and use gunship air support. I ran this by my boss and the Air America aviation unit and we all thought it was a great idea. It took a couple weeks to work up the scenario and get it scheduled but we were off and running.

On the day of the demonstration we moved the Cambodian battalion which was about ½ way through their advanced training to a side hill which allowed them to sit almost bleacher fashion overlooking our small arms range area. We placed with them several radios with speakers so they could monitor what was going on – the radio traffic was going to be in English but we had interpreters there to translate.

At the appointed hour two transport helicopters appeared from the direction of the South China Sea and discharged about 20 soldiers along with 2 seasoned USSF instructors well to the front and right of the observing Cambodian trainees. This unit soon came under fire, (all simulated of course), and called for air support. Air support soon arrived in the form of two Huey gunships.

The lead USSF instructor popped smoke to mark his position and asked the gunships to direct their fire to about 300 yards to his front. One gunship complied with a single White Phosphorus (WP) rocket to make sure they had the intended target.

Once this was established both gunships hammered the target with mini-guns and High Explosive (HE) rockets. The lead USSF instructor then called for the impact area to be moved closer and to the left to mop up the last remnants of the fictional enemy forces. The gunships responded "roger" and swung around for another pass.

While this was going on the PTTB executive officer and I were standing beside a jeep monitoring the radio exchanges between the gunships and the USSF instructor. We were about 200 yards to the rear of the Cambodian trainees.

The first gunship planted it's salvo of HE rockets in the new area indicated by the USSF instructor. The 2nd gunship lined up right behind it. I am not sure what happened because the next thing I saw and heard was at least one rocket impacting 5 yards in front of the Cambodian trainees and a huge surging backwards as they were either being blown rearward or just getting the hell out of the way – WTF just happened?

I immediately got on the horn (radio) and contacted the gunships and called for a ceasefire while at the same time rushing forward to ascertain the damage. As soon as we got on the scene it was obvious we had a big problem – dead, dying and wounded were lying all over the place. My next call was to the PTTB medical section to alert our one doctor and his staff that we had many wounded on the way. I then called the two slick helicopters who were still loitering in the area to come in to act as medevacs.

We loaded the wounded on choppers for the short ride to the PTTB helipad. The dead were loaded on a 2 ½ ton. Unfortunately most of the Cambodian leadership, to include the battalion commander and two of the company commanders were among the dead.

The battalion commander's 10 year old son who accompanied his father as the unit mascot was among the critically wounded. It took awhile but we finally cleared the area and marched the trainees back to their billeting area.

My next stop was the PTTB headquarters where we sent off a message to FANK headquarters in Bien Hoa. While this was going on the Cambodian Liaison Officer to PTTB was preparing his own notifications to his chain of command.

I then went to the dispensary where I saw the battalion commander's 10 year old son take his last breath. His body was cleaned, visible wounds were sewed up and he was laid beside his father. A total of 9 were killed and at least two dozen more were wounded.

What a tragic mess – a tragedy for the Cambodians and a mess for PTTB and Air America. What happened – how did this mishap occur?

FANK Training Command (FTC), our headquarters in Bien Hoa appointed an Article 32 officer who interviewed everyone involved. I still have copies of my statement.

The conclusion, based on statements from aviation munitions experts was that there was a malfunction of one of fins that stabilize the 2.75 HE rocket which made it veer off its intended path of flight. It was a tragic accident – one of many when men and machines play the game of war.

I continued as the operations officer for several more training cycles until I and a few others from FANK Training Command were hastily formed up into Mobile Training Teams (MTT) to help the ARVN plug the breach in the DMZ in what was later called the Easter Offensive.

Life goes on but I have always felt guilty for setting up that air support training scenario. I often wonder "Did I just kill 9 innocent people?"

Chapter 11

You Don't Want To Do That / Give Me The Gun!

This story took place during my 2nd tour (71-73) while I was the Operations Officer (S-3) of Phuoc Tuy Training Battalion (PTTB) with the mission of training Cambodians in Vietnam and returning them to Cambodia to fight their own war.

Once the Seabee unit came in to replace the electrical wires and plumbing the ARVN yanked out just before turning over their old NCO academy to us, we didn't live too badly.

No early lights out each evening to save the generators and no more using makeshift outhouses and the aroma of burning crap each morning. We even had a separate NCO club and officer's lounge. Neither did much business during the week but from time to time the unit hosted entertainment that was on the USO circuit. When that happened the officer's lounge shut down and the NCO club opened its doors to everyone.

Martha Raye (aka Colonel Maggie) visited us one weekend at Phuoc Tuy when this tale took place. I had met her once before on my 1st tour when she came to B-41 in Moc Hoa soon after my arrival, so I can claim I've swapped spit with her on two different occasions. I also had the honor of doing the same with Gypsy Rose Lee the queen of burlesque while at Moc Hoa. We also had some NFL players pay us a visit but I have no idea who they were – funny how all the ladies stick in your mind but the guys do not.

On the evening Martha Raye came to Phuoc Tuy just about all the Americans at PTTB were present at the NCO club for her comedy skit. She then sat down for a card game and some serious drinking with some of the senior NCO's. I'd seen this happen before and can attest to the fact that she had a "hollow leg" and could drink most folks under the table.

LTC G. was the PTTB commander. He had recently come to us when all of the battalion command slots had been upgraded from MAJ to LTC and the FTC command slot from LTC to COL. Most of us thought this was because the war was winding down and senior field grade officers were trying to get combat command time on their records.

LTC G. was a character. Some might say eccentric. Some might even call him something stronger. I know that I was not unhappy when they pulled me to head up the Armor MTT during the Easter Offensive.

Soon after Martha gave her skit and had retired to the poker game, LTC G. went back to his quarters which was actually a spacious reinforced bunker that had probably been the ARVN commandants HQ when the compound had been an ARVN NCO academy. The rest of us settled in for some serious drinking and conversation.

I was on my 2nd or 3rd "screwdriver" when there was the thunderous boom of a rifle shot somewhere in the wide open room that served as the NCO club. Everything went dead silent and folks were moving back from the opposite side of the room - WTF was going on?

Looking across the room I saw SSG S. standing with an M16 at port arms shouting "Where is he? – I'm going to kill that Mother fu*ker" I had no idea who he was talking about and it really didn't matter. I'm not sure what had led up to this but we were in a touchy situation. The way everyone had backed away it was obvious that no one had any desire to confront a madman with a gun.

I am not sure why, other than I was likely the senior person present, but I drained my drink, stood up and walked to the center of the room to confront SSG S. who was still cursing and calling for "that MF"

My first thought was to remain calm without saying anything that would instill a violent reaction. I walk directly to the front of SSG S. stopping about 2 feet from the menacing muzzle of the M16 and said in a calm voice "What's going on Sergeant S?"

He responded with "Where's the fu*king Colonel – I'm going to kill that MF SOB". Trying to remain calm, I moved in a little closer so that if he swung the muzzle toward me he'd have to step back. I said "The Colonel's not here and even if he was you don't want to do that". It went back and forth like this a couple times – other than our conversation, the room was dead silent. LTC G. was not well liked but I did not get into what had provoked SSG S. to this overt rage.

After what seemed like an eternity, but was probably only a minute or so, I held out my hand and said "Give me the gun". SSG S. hesitated a moment then passed the M16 to my outstretched hand.

With the weapon now in my hand I said in a more authoritative voice, "Sergeant S. as of right now you are confined to quarters". I than ordered the senior NCO present to organize a detail to accompany SSG S. to his quarters and remain with him until next morning when we could sort things out. Once this was accomplished I went to the bar and ordered another screwdriver.

The next morning several of us wrote statements which went with SSG S. to FANK HQ in Bien Hoa where he was court marshaled.

Post Script - Approximately 15 years later a MSG whom I did not recognize walked up to me at a gas station right outside of Ft Bragg, NC and said "I know who you are. You're the Captain who saved my life". I still couldn't place him until he said, "I'm SSG S." and then recounted the incident at Phuoc Tuy – it then all came back to me. He went on to say how, through hard work and determination, he had been able to overcome the blemish of a court marshal and had recently been promoted to MSG. Good for him!

I never did find out what had happened to provoke the incident – maybe it is just as well.

Swift Boats

In late 1968 I was assigned as the team leader of Special Forces team A-415 located just outside the hamlet of Tuyen Nhon near the top of IV Corps in the Mekong Delta. Tuyen Nhon was situated along a canal just off the Van Co Dong River. The general area was often referred to as "The Plain of Reeds". Everything north of the village of Tuyen Nhon and the canal where A-415 was located was designated a Free Fire Zone (FFZ). All friendly inhabitants had been removed from the area and relocated south of the canal.

The boundary line between South Vietnam and Cambodia in that area resembled a "Parrots Beak" or "Angels Wing" depending on how you looked at the map and was referred to as such. At that time Cambodia was off limits to any incursions by USA forces or our ARVN counterparts. The Viet Cong and the North Vietnamese Army had no such rule and took full advantage of Cambodia as their safe haven. Our mission was border surveillance, intelligence collection and interdiction of anyone traversing the FFZ.

Because Tuyen Nhon was located along a major river, the Van Co Dong, and had a PSP airstrip capable of landing C-123 aircraft we often collaborated with contingents of American units trying to take the fight to the enemy.

Shortly after I arrived at Tuyen Nhon we hosted a squadron or flotilla of USN aka "The Brown Water Navy or Swift Boats," and who set up on the canal just north of the CIDG family village along the PSP airstrip.

They were accompanied by a couple of flat bottomed landing craft with drop down ramps in the front. Our part of the mission was to furnish a reinforced platoon size unit (40-50 CIDG) as a reaction force or ground assault party for each of the landing craft that would accompany 2-4 Swift Boats as they went up and down the canals and rivers.

During the month or so that they were with us we had one group out all the time and the other either getting ready to go or just getting back. These excursions took place both during the day and at all hours of the night. Sometimes we were backed up by helicopters and sometimes not.

The general concept, especially at night was to go slowly up and down the waterways hoping the VC would be foolish enough to ambush the waterborne convoy. The Swift Boats would respond with overwhelming firepower while at the same time the landing craft would nudge into the bank, offload the reaction force which in theory would circle behind the VC so they could not escape. This worked pretty well the first few times we did it but like all things if you keep following the same playbook, the other team soon figures out how to score a few points as well.

On the evening 1-6-69 our senior communications man SSG J. and our junior medic PFC Dallas Padgett accompanied a reinforced CIDG platoon onto the landing craft to act as the reaction force as the Swift Boats motored up and down the Van Co Dong River hoping to flush out a VC ambush force.

PFC Padgett was on loan to us from MACV Team 85 because we were short medics. Team 85 was just getting established and was collocated with B-41 at Moc Hoa with no clear mission until they were fully staffed and could get their own compound built. Padgett was a good medic and we treated him just like all other members of the team to include taking his turn on patrols outside the wire.

(The next several paragraphs are as told to me by SSG J.) The Swift Boats and landing craft eased down the canal, past the CIDG village, the little hamlet of Tuyen Nhon and out into the Van Co Dong where it turned left in the direction of Moc Hoa. SSG J. and PFC Padgett were sprawled out on the upper deck of the landing craft and the CIDG were crammed in the lower deck.

The waterborne convoy had not gone far before all hell broke loose. B-40 rockets, machine guns and small arms fire erupted from the right bank. This was no small VC ambush – they obviously had been watching and had the routine figured out.

Three of the four Swift Boats were hit by B-40 rockets, two of them close enough to the waterline they had to quickly beach themselves on shore to avoid sinking. Everything, including the landing craft was raked with small arms fire.

The ambush was over almost as soon as it started. With two boats in danger of sinking and several USN and friendly indigenous wounded, there was no attempt to disembark the CIDG to encircle the enemy.

SSG J. and PFC Padgett had flattened themselves on the upper deck but were essentially unprotected from incoming fire. When the shooting subsided SSG J. turned to PFC Padgett and shouted "are you alright Dallas?" When there was no response he looked closer and saw that his companion was lying dead with lots of blood flowing from his neck.

The senior Swift Boat commander quickly took charge, off loaded the CIDG to set up a defensive perimeter around the beached boats and called for medevac to ferry the USN and CIDG wounded along with PFC Padgett's body to the nearest hospital.

While this was taking place the Swift Boat crews made temporary repairs to the holes near the waterline.

Here is a photo taken the next day of one of the boats which almost sank– those direct hits by VC fired B-40 rockets did some serious damage.

Eventually the Swift Boats and landing craft limped back up the canal and docked along the Tuyen Nhon airstrip.

There was a requirement for positive identification of each USA KIA so the following day I sent the A-415 XO to Saigon to verify it was indeed PFC Dallas Padgett.

A few days later I wrote the dreaded letter to his mother. We followed that with a package containing another letter proclaiming him an "Honorary Green

Beret" and enclosed a Green Beret and some of his personal effects.

We also make up a sign to hang over the dispensary proclaiming it to be the "Padgett Dispensary" and send her a photo.

PFC Padgett's mother and I exchanged a couple more letters because like all parents she wanted to know more about his last few days and final hour. She also attempted to correspond with SSG J. but to the best of my knowledge he did not respond.

What about the Swift Boats – well they stayed with us for a couple more weeks. They made repairs to the damaged boats and were soon back in operation. General Abrams came to visit them and I was invited to sit in on the visit. The visit was all about the Swift Boats and he did not once acknowledge that we provided the reaction force, adjacent airstrip and general security for the USN temporary base of operations.

One thing that changed was they no longer ran up and down the canals and rivers after dark. Most of our future operations consisted of amphibious insertions of our CIDG with the landing craft with sweeps circling back to the river or eventually being picked up by helicopters the Swift Boats frequently had assigned to them.

Chapter 13

Photo Story / Dallas Padgett's Time In Vietnam

In January 2016 right out of the blue I received an email with the subject line "Thank you for honoring Dallas Padgett". Rather than hit the delete button, as I do with a lot of unknown emails, I opened it up because PFC Padgett was a soldier who was killed while under my command at one of my Special Forces camps in 1969. After a few emails back and forth it turned out that R** & her cousin L** were younger cousins of PFC Dallas Padgett. R had seen my post while she was clicking through one of the Vietnam forums that honor our fallen from that era. They both asked questions and I ended up sending them the following photo story about Dallas Padgett's time in Vietnam. I've removed their full names and addresses to protect their privacy. Since that time we have become friends through social media and exchanged other information. What follows is my response to their questions.

(Beginning of letter sent to R & L)

I have assembled a photo story of what I think your cousin Dallas Padgett probably saw and experienced in Vietnam right up to the time he was killed in action (KIA) on January 6, 1969. The photos were taken by me - I had a 36mm camera and took a lot of photos. I'd send the film home and my wife would have it developed into slides because at the time slides were cheaper then glossy prints, plus everyone had a slide projector back in those days. I ended up with about 450 slides, none of which I saw until I came home. Like many things of that era they got relegated to the back of the drawer. Eventually the projector broke and I forgot about them until a few years ago when I found you could have slides converted to CD computer format. I took the whole bunch to Wal-Mart and had them converted for about $150.

I've looked, but unfortunately do not have any photos of Dallas. The best I can do is try to recreate what I think he may have seen. You have my permission to share this photo story with others.

It is likely that one of the first things Dallas saw after entering Vietnam and being assigned to a duty post was the city of Moc Hoa (Muck Waw) located about

75 miles south of Saigon in War Zone IV also known as the Mekong Delta Region. Moc Hoa was along the Van Co Dong River. Everything south of Saigon was flat. It was dry during the summer and very wet to the point of flooding during the winter or monsoon season.

Dallas was initially assigned to Military Assistance Command Vietnam (MACV) Advisory Team 85 which was co-located with Special Forces Detachment B-41 on the outskirts of Moc Hoa. B-41 was an intermediate headquarters for Special Forces camps located along the Vietnam / Cambodian border. The camp was named Camp George P. O'Toole in honor of Captain O'Toole who was KIA in 1967 at one of the outlying camps.

MACV Team 85 was just getting organized and did not have any outposts so I suspect Dallas worked awhile with the Special Forces medic at the B-41 dispensary as an assistant medic.

I was assigned to B-41 for a short while and then reassigned as the commander of Special Forces Camp A-415 Tuyen Nhon (Two-ee None). I am not sure if Dallas was already there when I arrived or maybe came at about the same time. Special Forces were always short medics so Dallas was on loan to us from MACV Team 85. He was a good medic and we treated him as a member of the team.

This was the view of A-415 Tuyen Nhon as you flew into camp.

The camp was only accessible by air or boat (No road connected it to anywhere other than a nearby village) this area was known as the "angel wing" or "parrots beak" because of how the boundary line between Vietnam and Cambodia looked on the map. At the time we could not legally enter into Cambodia.

This is the entrance to the camp as you come off the airstrip. The sign in Vietnamese reads in small print "Vietnam Army Special Forces" - larger print says Camp Tuyen Nhon.

Our mission was to monitor the boarder, collect intelligence and set up ambushes to interdict any infiltrators. All inhabitants north of the canal beside the camp had been moved out and the area declared a "free fire zone" which means anyone in there was considered hostile.

Each camp had a 12 man Vietnamese Special Forces team which was advised and assisted by a 12 man US Special Forces team. The soldiers were our equivalent of the National Guard, i.e.

locals organized into 3-4 companies totaling about 500 troops per camp.

The water tower in the distance was where water was piped in from the nearby canal, settled and treated for bacteria then filtered into a makeshift system to the main buildings within the compound.

The sand bags and metal drums you see stacked up were brought in as empty drums, split open to serve as reinforced walls which were filled with sand to absorb mortar and artillery fragments from entering critical areas whenever we came under enemy attack.

On the bottom right is a mortar pit which was our short range artillery when the camp came under attack.

Every Special Forces camp seemed to have a pet snake - we named ours Snuffy. From time to time we would send one of the local soldiers to the village to purchase a chicken which was placed in the cage. We then placed bets on how long the chicken would last. In the photo below snake tries to escape.

He was recaptured by our SF engineer (left) and our senior SF medic (right) Perry Browning, who was Dallas' supervisor. Perry was KIA about four months after this photo was taken.

We had a village right outside the gate. Our troops were "civilian soldiers" and brought their families along. The troop's official title was Civilian Irregular Defense Group (CIDG - much like our National Guard) There were lots of youngsters in that village. Dallas and his supervisor SSG Perry Browning were their source of medical care.

This little boy was born with a "hair lip". Our senior medic Perry Browning and Dallas worked a deal with higher headquarters where they arranged to send him and his mother to the Philippines to have the hair lip corrected. It made a very positive impression with the locals.

Our mission was border surveillance and making sure the North Vietnamese and Viet Cong did not infiltrate into the populated areas of South Vietnam. We kept folks in the field 24/7. Each operation was accompanied by 2 Americans. Everyone including our medics took their turn on patrols and ambush.

This is "yours truly" aka Captain K. with my Vietnamese radio operator in my younger days.

We often rode to war in "Huey" helicopters. As the commander, I liked to insert our troops as far out in our zone as possible. That way it took them at least two days to walk back to camp. This was a good way to insure they didn't just go outside of camp, settle down for a couple days and then walk back in saying they had not seen a thing which they tended to do if we did not have an American with them.

A thrill we all, including Dallas, shared was riding in the open door with our feet hanging out, flying into the unknown. We were young and dumb back then - safety was not a consideration.

We were on a major water way which allowed the US Navy "Swift Boats" or "Brown Water Navy" to visit us for joint operations. The theory was for them to go up and down the main river hoping to draw fire from shore. We had a reaction force following along in a converted landing craft which would land us just below the ambush and we would circle around behind the enemy to catch them between ourselves and the heavily armed boats. It was on an operation such as this that Dallas was killed.

I was not personally there when Dallas was killed but here is what happened. We paired up with the US Navy "Swift Boats" for a night run up and down the Van Co Dong River. Once again the idea was to draw fire and sweep in behind the enemy with our 50 man reaction force. It was SSG J**and PFC Dallas Padgett's time in the rotation to accompany them. They took off from the canal adjacent to our camp soon after dark and entered the main river.

Obviously the enemy had seen this maneuver before because they had not gone far when all hell broke loose. SSG J told me the next day that he and Dallas were on the upper deck of the landing craft which was a few feet higher than the lower portion where the troops were carried.

As soon as the firing started they both hit the floor of the deck but were essentially unprotected due its higher position. The boat drove on through the ambush site but any attempt to turn into the enemy was abandoned when it was learned two of the Swift Boats had also sustained serious hits.

(Photo below taken the day after ambush – note the large hole where the boat's number is suppose to be)

As soon as the boats were clear of the ambush John turned to Dallas and asked "Are you alright?" There was no answer so he turned to check and Dallas lay there motionless with blood pouring out of a wound to his neck area. A quick check revealed that Dallas was dead. Medevac helicopters were called to carry Dallas and several wounded to a hospital in Saigon.

PFC Dallas Padgett was the only American killed in my command during the two and one half years I served in Vietnam. He died a hero fighting for the preservation of freedom and the American ideals we hold so dear.

He was a good medic who was respected and loved by all. Although not officially in Special Forces we treated him as a member of the team. I remember writing the dreaded letter to his parents. We made him an "Honorary Green Beret" and sent a beret along with all the patches with the letter. I corresponded with his mother a couple times after that because like all parents she wanted details on his death.

We named the camp dispensary after Dallas. This dispensary was a special place just inside the front gate. It provided medical services not only to our soldiers but also their families. I watched our Special Forces medic Perry Browning and his able assistant Dallas Padgett treat some serious cases in this dispensary including the delivery of a couple babies. (End of letter sent to R&L)

This last photo shows PFC Padgett's final resting place. The photo was sent to me by one of his cousins.

The profile of PFC Dallas Padgett can be seen at http://www.virtualwall.org/dp/PadgettDL01a.htm

Chapter 14

Snake Eater

Most of the Special Forces camps in the Mekong Delta had a pet python snake. I'm not sure if this was because pythons were fairly common in that area or we just kept them to show how macho we were. There were numerous other snakes in the area to include the cobra, and the krait. The krait was jokingly referred to as the "two step snake", i.e. if it bit you you'd take two steps and fall over dead.

Other than pythons the only other snake I encountered was a large green snake resting on a large lily pad in an area used as a parachute drop zone (DZ) when I was assigned to B-41 in Moc Hoa. I was the B-41 S-1 and accepted my Vietnamese Special Forces (VNSF) counterpart's invitation to jump with him.

The jump itself was pretty wild – just throw on a parachute without any jumpmaster or riggers check, haul yourself into a Korean War vintage helicopter along with numerous VNSF soldiers. Once in the helicopter the jumpmaster pulled everyone's entire static line out and hooked it to a cable anchored on the wall of the helicopter – how we didn't end up becoming tangled in all those loose static lines only God knows. I was a happy paratrooper when we gained altitude and the jumpmaster tapped me with the "go" signal.

The opening shock, descent and landing were uneventful. We were jumping into a semi-dry rice paddy that had been secured by strategic stationing of local troops as the DZ. I'm sure some folks could tell a few tall tales and call it a combat jump but it wasn't – all I had for gear was my pistol belt and holstered 45.

Once I stuffed my chute in its kit bag, I was making toward the assembly area / parachute turn-in point when a large green snake hissed and slid off a lily pad right in front of me. It scared the hell out of me – I remember it to this day.

As previously mentioned most SF camps had a pet python. The first one I encountered was "Snuffy" at B-41(Moc Hoa). I have no idea how long Snuffy had been around but he was huge in diameter and about 12 feet long. When he had recently been fed he was fairly docile.

Most of us posed with him around our shoulders and neck. Looking back we were young and dumb and would have been in trouble if he had decided to "flex his muscles".

During my first tour (68-69) I was initially assigned as the B-team S-1 (Personnel / Administrative Officer for my non-military readers). As the S-1 I had the opportunity to visit all of the subordinate SF camps and most had one or two pythons penned up in a wire cage. Some were longer than Snuffy but none had his girth. None appeared to be as "tame" either.

When I was re-assigned as the team leader of A-415 (Tuyen Nhon) one of our favorite distractions was to give Mamasan enough piaster's to purchase a chicken which was thrown in with our snake. We would then throw a dollar in the pot and draw numbers to coincide with x hours before the chicken became a huge bulge in the snake's body – the lucky number won the pot.

Meat, other than fish, for the locals was expensive and always in short supply. A source of "free meat" was the large rats that burrowed into the dikes that formed the rice paddies. I am not sure if they were a smaller version of North American muskrats or a larger version of our common rat. In any case it was not unusual to see some of our off duty CIDG walking the dikes with a long bamboo pole tipped with a 3 prong gig. They would sit with the gig poised over a hole waiting for the rat to emerge – very similar to Eskimos before they swapped the spear for a gun. Another source of "free meat" was the python.

I accompanied a company of CIDG on a sweep through some elephant grass to a suspected VC village that had been abandoned because the area had recently been sprayed with defoliant -

now called Agent Orange. The spraying had taken place about a month prior and I remember thinking, "this place looks like the face of the moon". Areas that had received a good dose of the defoliant were devoid of any green vegetation. Everything was black. There were a few old burial plots which stood out like a sore thumb. It was obvious that no one was coming back here to live for quite some time.

The CIDG soldiers were lifting, probing and searching for anything left behind as we made our way through the abandoned village. I was with the company commander a little to the rear when all of a sudden there was shooting and shouting coming from our lead platoon. Naturally the first thing that comes to mind is "here we go again – we are going to earn our combat pay today".

The radio stated crackling and the company commander broke into a big grin and started talking so fast that I could not follow what was going on even though I had been the honor graduate at the one year Vietnamese language school I had attended prior to being assigned to Vietnam. All I could make out was "lớn" – big something but I was not sure what. Things slowed down and the interpreter said "No VC – soldiers find big snake".

By this time the shooting had stopped but there was still a lot of shouting as we made our way to where the action was. The first thing I saw was 3-4 soldiers on their hands and knees franticly digging while several more were pulling the wriggling body of a very large python from a hole. Once the snake was clear of the hole another soldier gave it 2 quick shots to the head – it still trashed around quite awhile.

Once the excitement was over the story finally came out. The CIDG had been soldiering for a lot time and obviously knew where to look and what to look for. They had come upon several crocks or barrels of rice buried under what appeared to be the fire-ring of an open kitchen. Obviously someone had planned or hoped to come back for it later. However, "Mr. Big Snake" had found it and taken up residence where the eating was good.

I would have loved to have seen the expression of the first soldier's face as he was digging up what he thought was a hidden barrel of rice.

It took me a while to comprehend what they intended to do with a 15 foot dead python. The interpreter explained to me that it contained many pounds of good meat and the troops who had "captured it" had no intention of leaving it behind.

One of them draped it over his shoulders and we continued with our sweep. Nothing else of significance was found.

This was a Free Fire Zone, meaning anyone found in it was considered hostile, so we burned what was left of the abandoned village.

You should have seen the wide eyed looks of the helicopter crew when we tried to jump on with a 15 foot dead python. Both the crew chief and the pilot initially said "no way". I did a little sweet talk and promised them some souvenir loot so they finally relented.

The door gunner kept staring at the snake all the way back to camp. I think if it had contracted the way dead snakes sometimes do he would have yanked the M-60 out of it's pedestal and shot the floor out of the helicopter.

Big doings when we got back to camp. They had to parade the snake around for everyone to see and tell and re-tell the story. Two days later I was the guest of honor where I was served some of the finest soup I have ever eaten.

"Yep – I am a genuine snake eater"

Chapter 15

Big Fight – Many Dead

I have to set the stage for this story which took place in early summer 1969 at Thanh Tri (A-414). What occurred was my small connection to what is referred to as "The Green Beret Affair" which has been the subject of 2-3 books and the same number of movies. The unraveling of The Green Beret Affair originated at Thanh Tri, moved to the South China Sea, MACV HQ, Long Bien Jail, the National Press and the White House.

To get a feel for what occurred from the perspective of those on the ground I encourage you to watch the documentary film "Double Agent Down – The Green Beret Affair" written and produced by Terry McIntosh, now available for free viewing at https://youtu.be/1gE3g-4K-ng.

In the early spring of 1969 the B-41 Commander LTC H. was not happy with things at Thanh Tri. I am not sure exactly what the problem was but his direction to me was "get those guys outside the wire or he would find someone who could". He also made it clear that he was not talking about the CIDG. His decision to have me make a lateral move as team leader from Tuyen Nhon (A-415) to Thanh Tri (A-414) probably had something to do with me not getting along with my VNSF counterpart at Tuyen Nhon.

The fellow I replaced at Thanh Tri was reassigned as the assistant to S-3 or S-2 at B-41. The team sergeant soon made the same move. The VNSF commander at Thanh Tri was also switched out the same week I arrived. He was replaced by a hard charging VNSF Dại uý and we were off and running.

One of the first things we did was institute a policy of sending at least one USSF with any platoon or company size operation.

This caused a little mumbling by some of the USSF not wanting to push the odds because they considered themselves "short timers". The only problem with this theory was that with a one year tour and often an initial assignment to the C or B team, everyone could be considered "short timers" by the time they were assigned to an A team. Everyone, including myself and the team sergeant went into the rotation. The story which is about to unfold took place about 30 days before my replacement arrived.

As mentioned in previous stories one of my favorite ways to insure we were covering our sector was to insert the troops some distance from camp when we had helicopters available. That way they had at least a 2-3 day walk back even if they returned in a straight line – longer if they zig-zagged to check out key terrain features. This ploy kept them from going just out of sight of camp and setting up for 2-3 days and returning with nothing to report.

In late May or early June of 1969 we inserted a CIDG company accompanied by 2 VNSF and 2 USSF (1LT W. & SFC M.) to the far end of our sector where it tied in with Tuyen Nhon (A-415). Their mission was to remain just south of the Cambodian border and set up ambushes as they made their way back to camp.

On the afternoon of the 2nd day of what was expected to be a 3 day operation we heard what sounded like a significant firefight taking place some distance to the east of Thanh Tri.

We did not have any radio traffic from our USSF but the camp commander had a short garbled transmission from his VNSF indicating they were in contact - then the radio went dead.

I alerted B-41, our higher HQ, that one of our units was in contact and asked them to line up some aviation support while we tried to figure out what was going on.

Two hours later a bedraggled looking CIDG soldier came running from the general area where we had earlier heard gunfire. Before he made it to the entrance of the compound another soldier was seen running our way some distance behind him. As soon as these two individuals made the perimeter there was a lot of shouting and confusion.

Once they calmed down the gist of what they were saying was **"BIG FIGHT – MANY DEAD"**.

While this was going on we had not heard anything over the USSF radio band we kept open so we could talk to our men in the field. The camp commander said he was sporadically getting something from his VNSF radio but it was confusing and he still did not know what was going on.

After we talked with the two CIDG stragglers who had ran back into camp with only their uniforms but no weapons or web gear, it was obvious we had the makings of a disaster on our hands.

I reestablished contact with B-41 in Moc Hoa and asked them for sufficient helicopter support to airlift a minimum of a reinforced platoon to go the aid of – I really didn't know what. I also asked them to get their USAF FAC up in the air and have him get some close air support "fast movers" on standby. By this time, the sun was about to go down so I also asked for a flare ship to be on standby. While I was lining up these assets the VNSF executive officer mustered our Combat

Recon Platoon (CRP) and got them heading towards the helipad.

The VNSF commo room finally started to make sense of what was coming across the radio. The camp commander Dia-uy Diem took over the radio and after a bit said one of the USSF wanted to talk with me.

I got on the horn and it was SFC M. He said "We were caught in a devastating ambush. There was lots of confusion and everyone started running to the rear. We finally got them stopped and I've sit up a hasty perimeter. We have a lot of wounded – I'm not sure how many dead. The enemy seems to have withdrawn because there is no more firing. I'm trying to hold things together but we need help". He did not mention, as I later learned, that he himself had been wounded or that 1LT W. was missing.

With that information we got a company of CIDG saddled up and on the way to the helipad where the CRP was already locked and loaded. At the same time I apprised the B-41 Operations Officer (S-3) of our situation and asked for helicopters and AF assets as soon as possible. He told me they were on the way.

The VNSF executive officer and I grabbed a radio, our weapons and web gear and headed to the helipad just outside the front gate.

Our helipad could accommodate 8-10 helicopters at a time and was likely envisioned as an airstrip when originally built but because things flooded often the soil was unstable and no fixed wing aircraft ever attempted to land while I was there. We soon had sufficient choppers inbound to accommodate the entire reaction force.

The VNSF XO and I jumped in the lead bird along with our shared radio operator and we were soon airborne and heading into who knows what with 8-10 choppers filled with scared but determined CIDG troops right behind us.

We headed in the general direction where we assumed the beleaguered CIDG had hunkered down. It was dark by this time so I asked SFC M. to pop a single flare as soon as he heard us in his vicinity. Once we saw the flare we made an approach and landed 2-3 helicopters at a time in a landing zone marked by flashlights and cigarette lighters.

We landed without incident which was good because everyone had been prepared for the VC to greet us with small arms and mortar fire. The VNSF XO and I were the first on the ground and placed the follow on troops into a perimeter with what was left of the decimated CIDG unit in the center.

As soon as I located SFC M. the first thing I noticed was his leg was wrapped in a bloody bandage. SFC M. assured me he was OK for the moment and was trying to hold things together. I then looked around for 1LT W. but could not see him. When I asked about him SFC M. said "I don't know. We got separated in the confusion and I have not seen him since all hell broke loose and we were forced to withdraw to this location". He went on to say "we have lost several men and many of those still with us are without weapons". I looked around and saw several wounded CIDG in a makeshift aid station. The whereabouts of 1LT W. was uncertain. He was either lying out there wounded or dead – or had been captured by the VC.

First things first – we made sure the perimeter was secure and then called for multiple medevacs. We placed SFC M. on the last chopper out and wished him luck. That is the last time I ever saw him. Fifty years later I can't remember if I put him in for a valor award or not. I hope I did, he certainly deserved it. By the standards back then he merited a Bronze Star for Valor. With today's inflated award system it would have been a Silver Star or higher.

By the time the last medevac was out of the way we had a USAF C-130 gunship overhead. I told him we didn't need his firepower at the moment but could sure use any flares he might have to help light things up. He replied "No problem – I've got a full load of flares and if we ration them out they will keep you in "daylight" for as long as I have fuel. I can stick with you for 3-4 hours".

With the C-130 gun ship providing cover, and flares lighting up the area, we decided to fan out in a double line of scrimmages and walk back through the ambush site to make sure there were no more wounded lying there. Of course we were also hoping to recover our dead.

It did not take long to locate discarded weapons and web gear. Soon a shout announced a dead body was found and then another and another. I personally went to the site of each of these grisly discoveries expecting to see the body of 1LT W. but instead observed one of our CIDG soldiers. We located 7 CIDG KIA. We laid them out adjacent to what later became the command post and set about establishing a tight perimeter.

Our helicopter support was long gone and would not return until the following morning. Our FAC had run low on fuel and returned to Moc Hoa and would not be returning unless we ran into trouble.

The C-130 gunship continued to circle and drop flares. The pilot and I had a good conversation. He was real apologetic as he announced he was running low on fuel and had to return to base. By then it was 2-3 o'clock in the morning so we just settled in for the night.

After conferring with the CIDG company commander and my VNSF counterpart we concluded that 2 men were unaccounted for – 1LT W. and one CIDG soldier who had been acting as his radio operator.

With all the emotion and activity I did not have to pop a "green weenie" to stay awake. Every time I thought about nodding off I'd look over at the pile of dead bodies and was immediately wide awake.

About an hour after the C-130 left and we were engulfed in total darkness there was a commotion on one side of the perimeter. We all went on full alert. The first thing I thought was "Here we go – we have VC probers and are about to be attacked and maybe overrun".

There was more confusion and then the word was passed that 1LT W. and the missing CIDG were coming through the lines. I was certainly relieved but was also thinking "GD where has he been".

Before long 1LT W. was brought to the command group area and I asked him for a full report. He related that when they came under ambush he and the radio operator hit the ground and by the time the firing had subsided the CIDG had withdrawn so he and his radio operator had hunkered down and hoped for the best.

He seemed pretty withdrawn and non-committal so I did not press the issue. I could understand why he was not saying much. We were laying beside 7 dead who only hours before had been full of aspirations for a long life. We still had to get through the rest of the night.

Daylight came without anymore incidents or excitement. While we were waiting for helicopters to give us a lift back to camp we once again formed up into scrimmages and went back through the ambush site. We located a couple more discarded CIDG weapons and web-gear. It appeared the VC had sprung the ambush and then immediately withdrawn across the Cambodian border where in early 1969 we could not legally pursue in accordance with the rules of engagement.

B-41 could only muster 4 helicopters for our extraction. We had the better part of 2 companies of CIDG on the ground so we were going to have to set up a perimeter and be picked up about 50 at a time – it was going to take 2-3 lifts with a 30 minute turnaround time.

We sent the majority of the company that got mauled in the ambush, along with their dead out on the first lift. 1LT W. seemed eager to get out of there so I let him go as well.

It took two more lifts by the 4 choppers to get us all back to Thanh Tri. We cheated by overloading the birds with one extra "little people", 12 being the normal load.

Even at that we couldn't get them all on in 3 lifts – if you read one of my other short stories "Riding to War in a Huey" you may recall that we had a brave pilot who lifted us off with 16 "little people" on board.

The VNSF XO and I were both glad to see the Thanh Tri helipad come into view but our work was not done for the day. He had to make sure the troops secured all their gear before being released. There were also death notices to deliver – at least half the KIA had families living in the CIDG dependent village.

I went by the camp dispensary where some of the lightly wounded were being treated. The KIA were also there being cleaned up and made presentable for release to their families The more seriously wounded had been flown directly to a ARVN hospital. Once these things were checked on it was time to prepare a written report for transmission to our headquarters, B-41 in Moc Hoa.

A few days later the VNSF Camp Commander Dia-uy Diem and I attended a Buddhist funeral ceremony where the KIA, wrapped tightly in body bags were laid on individual pyres of wood. Once the monk was done with his part, one of our CIDG sloshed diesel fuel on each body bag and down onto the wood. The camp commander and I were each given a lit torch and walked from pyre to pyre, lighting all 7 and then stood back as each body was consumed in flames.

Yes indeed, **"BIG FIGHT - MANY DEAD"**

Chapter 16

Flatter Than a Pancake

I've previously written about how Special Forces "A" teams were on their own for chow or rations and how we begged and bartered "war souvenirs" with American units for rations. We had plenty of captured weapons but I don't recall that we ever captured a VC flag.

Have no fear; the SF mind can be cunning and creative at times. One of our housekeepers had a sewing machine and was good with needle and thread so we had her sew up a few flags. Add some chicken blood, a few bullet holes and then soil it with dirt and you had a genuine VC flag captured in a fierce battle. All you needed now was a good storyteller and a gullible rear echelon logistics guy looking for a souvenir.

Many food items such as dehydrated eggs, powdered milk, flour and pancake mix, all of which came in big OD cans, did not even require bartering. There seemed to be lots of it – all we needed to do was ask. These aforementioned items were the staple of our morning meals. To help give the pancakes that "taste of home" our Vietnamese cook would drop a couple of maple flavored pills in some boiling water laced with a liberal amount of sugar – that concoction was a little watery but it was the US Army's version of maple syrup.

I'd just been transferred from Tuyen Nhon (A-415) to Than Tri (A-414). We had basically the same diet at both camps. I was busy trying to get the feel of a new team. The Moc Hoa (B-41) commander LTC H. had mandated "get those guys outside the wire or I will find someone who will" so my emphasis was not on the consistency of the pancakes.

After a little grumbling and a couple significant personnel changes we started earning our hostile fire pay - but what about the pancakes?

The pancakes at Than Tri were rubbery and thin. We joked they could have been used as blow-out patches on the camp's 2 ½ ton truck. I don't recall the pancakes at Tuyen Nhon being, no pun intended, "flatter than a pancake".

They were so bad that we even looked forward to the days when powdered scrabble eggs were on the menu. Both camps were using the same pancake mix so it must have been different cooking styles.

My room was 2 doors down from the main room or open area in the team house – we had a radio speaker and mike wired into that room which was where someone from the team pulled watch during off hours.

At the far end of the common area was a divider which separated the kitchen or cooking area from the common area. I was an early riser and often drank a cup of coffee and worked on administrative duties while the rest of the team was waking up and the cooks were preparing breakfast. This close proximity to the kitchen also allowed me to get "first dibs" on a biscuit or whatever else might be on the menu.

One morning I smelled the sweet aroma of sugar water and heard the opening of big cans so knew we were in for the dreaded blow-out patches which were masquerading as pancakes.

I went back for another cup of coffee and sure enough the cook's helper was opening a second large can of mix. It took at least two cans and maybe more to feed the entire team. While I watched I saw the cook's helper toss a small white paper packet that was on top of the pancake mix into the trash. I assumed it was some sort of "desiccant" inserted in things to suck up the moisture.

Being nosey I walked over and pulled it out of the trashcan and low and behold it was a paper envelope of baking powder. A close reading of the instructions revealed you were supposed to thoroughly mix the contents into each can of mix as part of the recipe for pancakes.

I spoke some Vietnamese, having gone to language school prior to becoming a full fledged Green Beret, but I wanted to make sure, so solicited one of our interpreters to ask the cook if the baking powder had been discarded by mistake. The answer was they had been discarding it all along.

It took a little coaching but I finally convinced them to try mixing it in with the flour. They didn't like doing it and muttered they knew how to cook and Dia-uy must be dinky-dau.

To our surprise the pancakes started to rise and no longer had that rubbery, "blow-out patch" consistency. They were so good that everyone had 2nd and 3rd helpings and folks began looking forward to pancakes on the menu.

It's funny how little things like that can be big morale boosters.

Chapter 17

"Walk in the Sun"

Now that 51 years have passed hopefully I can tell this story without someone knocking on my door. If you recall from some of my other stories you know that most of the Special Forces camps were set up along the Vietnam / Cambodia / Laos border. Our mission was to monitor what was going on along the border. We also conducted patrols and set up ambushes to deter the VC and NVA from infiltrating into Vietnam.

The civilian population had been moved from the most of the border and the area north of the SF camps was designated a "Free Fire Zone" - meaning anyone found in there was considered hostile until proven otherwise. At the time I was there in 1968-69 we were not allowed to go into Cambodia. The VC and NVA did not abide by the same rule and used Cambodia as a safe haven or sanctuary from which to launch operations. One such operation was the deadly ambush written about earlier, titled "Big Fight – Many Dead"

That ambush was the first significant bloodying of the CIDG at Thanh Tri (A-414) in quite some time and infuriated the relatively new LLDB (VNSF) commander Dại uý Diem and the camp's CIDG because it was their friends and fellow soldiers lying in a hospital or atop a burning funeral pyre.

I was a short-timer by any standard used to check off time left in-country prior to getting on the "freedom bird", lifting off and heading home. I could count the days left by ticking off my fingers and pulling off my boots – I might even have a couple toes left over.

My replacement was rumored to be at our immediate headquarters, B-41 in Moc Hoa. That did not stop me when Dại uý Diem proposed an operation to locate, fix and engage the enemy force responsible for our recent deadly debacle. Dại uý Diem had his own intelligence gathering network and professed to know exactly where to find these folks. Being young and dumb I said "Hell yes, let's do it".

We loaded two CIDG (Civilian Irregular Defense Group) companies and the CRP (Combat Recon Platoon) with a double basic load of small arms ammo plus all the 60mm mortars in the camp. No helicopter insertion this time. I asked Dại uý Diem if he wanted helicopters but he declined telling me it would be better to surprise the enemy by appearing to go for a typical CIDG "walk in the sun".

Out the front gate we went headed in an easterly direction. The CRP took the lead in an abbreviated wedge formation with the two CIDG companies to the left and right rear, each in a similar wedge formation.

Dại uý Diem, our jointly shared interpreter and I made up the command group near the head of one of the CIDG companies. Our interpreter was actually Dại uý Diem's admin assistant / body guard. She was easy on the eyes and could handle an M-16 as well as the CIDG soldiers.

We didn't really need the interpreter because Dại uý Teiu spoke fluent English and I spoke and understood Vietnamese as long as the conversation was not going too fast. I interacted real well with both of the CIDG company commanders so had my interpreter accompany the other USSF who positioned himself with the CRP platoon leader.

We walked eastward all day parallel to the Vietnamese / Cambodian border without incident. The border in that area was not marked but I estimate we were about 15 kilometers south of the border. Just before setting up a defensive position for the evening we turned northward and set up in an area I recognized as near the location of the deadly ambush only a couple weeks prior. I hoped the Dại uý knew what he was doing. I didn't get much sleep that night.

The following morning Dại uý Diem conferred with the CRP platoon leader and then turned and said it would be better if the other USSF stayed with us at the command group. He then sent the CRP north to get a better fix on the border area.

About noontime a squad of them came back all excited and had a rapid conversation with Dại uý Teiu. I couldn't follow it all but figured out they had found the enemy and had left half the platoon there to keep track of them.

We cautiously followed the CRP squad to just a bit short of where the rest of the platoon was hunkered down and observing what appeared to be a village. There was no canal, river or markers to show that just to our front was the Vietnam / Cambodia border but it was fairly obvious to be the case.   Dại uý

Diem and I pulled out binoculars and watched for awhile.

It was soon revealed to be more of a training camp than a village. It was predominantly populated with males with very few females or "mama-sans". I did not see any children. Most of the males were armed and several appeared to be in a training class, perhaps teaching them to disassemble and maintain their weapons. Another thing that I find comical to this day is after we had been watching about a half hour 20-30 males marched on the scene doing what appeared to be dismounted drill. We were obviously watching a VC/NVA training camp that felt safe on the Cambodian side of the border.

At this stage it was definitely Dại uý Diem's show. I was just an advisor and I don't think he wanted nor needed advice. My tongue was likely also silenced by the recent memory of collecting friendly dead and setting fire to their funeral pyres. These enemy combatants had inflicted those casualties on us and then withdrawn to their safe sanctuary only a couple weeks prior. For Dại uý Diem and the CIDG it was payback time.

We moved both CIDG companies up on line and withdrew the CRP platoon to our rear to act as rear security. This was done with as much stealth as possible and thankfully we were not discovered. By this time it was late afternoon. Most of the activity at the enemy camp had ceased and they appeared to be settling in for the evening. I noticed that all our 60mm mortars and ammunition were consolidated just to our rear under the control of one of the LLDB (VNSF).

The CIDG troops were armed with recently acquired M16 rifles but we had retained our thirty caliber machine guns and BAR's – these were consolidated in two spots closely supervised by a trusted NCO from each CIDG company. I wasn't sure what was going to happen next.

At about dusk Dại uý Diem spoke into his radio and there was the thunk, thunk, thunk of 60mm mortars spewing multiple rounds of high explosive skyward in an arch toward the enemy encampment. Before those projectiles landed the machine guns and BAR's opened up.

They were soon joined by M16 rifles on fully automatic. We were a good four or six hundred yards from the camp so I am not sure how effective the M16's were but the tracer rounds from the machine guns and BAR's were pouring plunging fire right into the heart of our target.

It was over almost before it began. As soon as the 60mm mortars were running low on ammunition Dại uý Diem barked into the radio again and we began to withdraw. The CRP platoon faded right and left to allow the CIDG companies to move deeper southward into Vietnam. There was some confusion when we began to take return fire from the enemy but the CRP put a stop to that.

We moved rapidly to the rear until it became too dark to see and then set up a reinforced perimeter for the night. The VC/NVA followed us but they didn't know our strength. They were reluctant to try more than a couple probes which were met with a lot of return fire. They faded back across the border before dawn.

It took most of the next day to walk back to Thanh Tri. Everyone was in high spirits. We had taken it to the enemy without suffering a casualty of our own. The folks we had given a bloody nose were probably the same ones who had recently done the same to us. I guess you could say we had regained our honor.

I'm not sure how Dại uý Diem reported things to his chain of command. Me – I reported it as just another "walk in the sun".

My replacement CPT Louis Geneseo was on site when I returned to camp. We did an inventory of everything I was signed for and made the trip to Can Tho where he assumed responsibly for it and I was relieved of that responsibly – then back to Moc Hoa where LTC Beck gave him his marching orders and shook my hand and slapped me on the back for a "job well done".

Unfortunately less than two weeks later, Dại uý Diem, the best LLDB (VNSF) I ever worked with, my replacement, CPT Geneseo and my old boss LTC Beck were all dead. They, along with several others were killed in a tragic helicopter crash in the same area where this story took place. God took many innocent souls that day. I hope their families were able to cope and move on from that terrible time.

Chapter 18

The Armor MTT at Hue / Phu Bai

In the spring of 1972 the NVA pushed the ARVN off the DMZ in what was soon to be labeled The Easter Offensive. The push southward was easier then the NVA had anticipated and like so many such offensives it soon petered out when they over extended their supply lines just south of HUE.

During the ARVN's hasty retreat two infantry divisions and one heavy tank regiment was decimated. Once the City of Hue was retaken and ARVN lines stabilized with massive aerial and ground assistance from the United States, USAV/MACV called upon the HQ of FANK Training Command to use its SF assets to form up MTT's to rush to the Hue / Phu Bai area to assist with reorganizing and retraining the decimated ARVN units.

At the time I was the Operations Officer (S-3) at Phuoc Tuy Training Battalion (PTTB). Our mission was training Cambodians and shipping them back to Cambodia. I was also an armor officer – back in the days before SF became a branch officers retained their original specialty in addition to becoming SF qualified. A handful of others along with myself were told at about noontime to pack our combat gear – we were told nothing else. We were on our way by ¾ ton truck at 1500 for the 1 ½ hour drive to Bien Hoa.

Once in Bien Hoa we linked up with 25-30 other senior NCO's and a few officers. Someone briefed us on the disaster up near the DMZ and told us we would be put on a plane the next day. Our destination was where the line still held just a little south of the city of Hue.

Our mission was to help reorganize and retrain the ARVN for the push back to the DMZ. They then broke us down by specialty into 3 mobile training teams, 2 infantry and 1 armor. I was designated the OIC of the armor team.

As you might expect the pucker factor and rumor mill kicked in. I'd been in-country for almost a year on this, my 2nd tour, and being the S-3 was fairly well connected with the folks at Bien Hoa but I still did not know what was going on or what to expect. I do recall there was a lot of weapons' cleaning while we waited for our plane the next morning.

My Armor MTT consisted of myself and 8-9 men who could tell the difference between a 2 ½ ton truck and a tank. None of us, including two Armor Branch 1LT's had any recent armor experience.

We landed at an airfield just outside of Hue / Phu Bai which was now a major ARVN headquarters. This was also where the two decimated infantry divisions and the tank regiment had stopped after being driven off the DMZ.

My team was quartered in an old MACV compound and the two infantry MTT's were quartered elsewhere. The base had recently been turned over to the ARVN by the 101st Air Mobile before their departure as a part of the USA drawdown.

The next day the MACV Armor Advisor for I Corps arrived with a ¾ ton truck which I had to sign for. He then took us to where the remains of the 20th ARVN Tank Regiment were located.

When the 20th had been on the DMZ they had 54 M-48 tanks and about 300 men. When we were introduced to what remained of the regiment they had 4 tanks and about 100 men. Obviously, our task included more than a little refresher training.

The regimental commander, an ARVN colonel, told us that many of his missing troops were filtering back into the ranks and he expected he'd only need 75-100 replacements for troops killed or wounded – he was working on that through ARVN headquarters.

The replacement of 50 tanks was entirely another matter. The MACV Armor Advisor told us there were no replacement tanks readily available in-country. They would be coming one at a time via C-5A aircraft from the states with the 1st due to arrive in about a week. This gave us time to work up a plan to get the 20th ARVN Tank Regiment back into the fight.

The Armor MTT put it's collective head together and came up with a training program that consisted of tank related maintenance, communications, driving skills, use of machine gun and main gun on various targets and maneuvers.

We also made up a tentative plan to receive and process the replacement tanks and related equipment as they arrived. By the end of the first week we were ready to go.

As with all MTT's where you rely upon the host nation to provide troops and equipment at a certain place on a certain time there were a few hiccups but for the most part it went pretty well.

The Commander of the 20th ARVN Tank Regiment spoke good English, having recently graduated from the Armor Officers Carrier Course at Ft Knox, KY. He and I got along very well.

We agreed that we'd concentrate on forming up, equipping and training one company at a time. Two of the three tank company commanders had survived the hasty withdrawal from the DMZ so this worked out well.

After about a month one company was ready to return to duty. The 2nd company returned to the line two weeks later. The 3rd company which had a new commander and at least 50% new soldiers took a lot longer – there was also the challenge of obtaining replacement tanks one at a time.

The Armor MTT remained at Hue / Phu Bai helping reorganize, re-equip and retrain the 20th ARVN Tank Regiment for a total of 87 days. It has been close to 50 years now but It was an adventure. Some things stand out in my memory like they happened yesterday.

We were billeted in an old MACV compound which was actually within the perimeter of the airfield. Security was provided by the ARVN. Because we were within the inner perimeter we did not experience any direct attacks but had to scurry to bunkers at least every other night when the base itself came under attack. I recall one night the ammo dump was hit and set fire. The fire moved through the entire stock of various munitions which gave us a better fireworks show than any 4th of July celebration.

One of the tank companies we sent back to the fight encountered two NVA Russian built tanks. In the tank battle that followed one NVA tank was destroyed and the other captured.

The captured tank, along with other NVA heavy weapons was brought back to our location for examination and documentation. The tank was eventually sent to Saigon to help make the case that the Russians were assisting the NVA.

One of our tasks was helping train new drivers. I will never forget the morning we placed a new driver in a tank along with several others hanging onto the outside to observe. The driver put the tank in reverse instead of forward. In the confusion and shouting to correct the situation the driver got excited, floored the accelerator, and backed into a wooden barracks building.

All but one of the half dozen ARVN soldiers who were riding on the rear was able to jump clear before the tank backed into and through the building. The unlucky ARVN soldier who didn't jump was squashed like a bug. He was wearing a "steel pot" that remained on his head but smashed to half it's size. There are some images you will never forget!

About 4 weeks into the training we were visited by a USA Brigadier General from USAV. I had interacted with this BG before when he visited PTTB where I had been the S-3. He had a reputation for being fair but volatile if he thought you were BS'ing or not trying hard enough to solve a challenge.

The I Corps MACV Senior Armor Advisor was present – I'm not sure what he said to the BG but next thing I heard was "MAJOR, you're not in my chain of command but in addition to being the USAV G-3 I'm a senior advisor to the

Commanding General MACV. I'm going to have your ass out of here before the sun sets". Well as it turns out the BG didn't make the "sun set" deadline but the Major was gone 48 hours later.

Towards the end of the Armor MTT's 87 day existence the city of Hue was back in ARVN hands and secure enough for the 20th ARVN Tank Regiment Commander and I to tour the city and enjoy a restaurant meal of fried frog legs and beer.

Once the 20th was up and back into the fight the Armor MTT was disbanded with the team members going back to their original assignments with FANK, training Cambodians.

My S-3 job at PTTB had been assumed by another captain and the Cambodian program was being phased out. I remained at Bein Hoa to write the Armor MTT After Action Report and further assignment as the S-3 of FANK. The FANK mission was evolving from training Cambodians to providing MTT's to the ARVN throughout the entire country. Soon after taking that job I was rushed back to Hue/Phu Bai to temporally replace one of the infantry MTT commanders who had to go on emergency leave.

We finished up at Hue/Phu Bai and moved the MTT, via VC controlled Highway 1 down to Da Nang for a continuation of the MTT mission. That ride down Highway 1 was an adventure described in my next short story.

Thankfully I was soon recalled to Bien Hoa to resume my S-3 duty of helping phase out the Cambodian program and manage the MTT missions.

Chapter 19

The Fire Engine at Da Nang

This took place in 1972 soon after we had finished up with re-training the ARVN 20th Tank Regiment which had been decimated when they had been pushed off the DMZ at the beginning of what was labeled the Easter Offensive. That period has already been the subject of another short story titled **"87 *days with the Armor MTT at Hue / Phu Bai*"**.

Once the 20th Tank Regiment was back in the fight, the Armor MTT was disbanded and personnel returned to their original mission of training Cambodians.

Prior to being tasked to head up the Armor MTT I had been the S-3 or operations officer at Phuoc Tuy, one of the three Cambodian Training Battalions under the FANK program.

In my absence my assistant filled in for me. The Cambodian program was being phased out so I was reassigned as the S-3 at FANK Headquarters in Bien Hoa. In addition to closing out the Cambodian program FANK was now tasked to provide refresher training to the ARVN in anticipation of our complete withdrawal from Vietnam.

Soon after taking that job I was rushed back to Hue/Phu Bai to temporally replace one of the infantry MTT commanders who had to go on emergency leave. We finished up at Hue/Phu Bai and moved the MTT, via Highway 1 down to Da Nang in borrowed ¾ ton trucks for a continuation of the MTT mission.

I remember the ride down Highway 1 very well. The road was not exactly "clear" by American standards but what the hell, we were Special Forces and didn't exactly adhere to what the rest of the US Army, who had already cased their colors and headed home, called standard protocol. The road had a poor reputation. It traversed several narrow mountain passes which had been the scene of earlier ambushes.

All the bridges had been destroyed, rebuilt or bypassed on numerous occasions.

The pucker factor was high but after a few stops and starts along with a lot of explanation and ID checking at ARVN checkpoints, we emerged on the outskirts of Da Nang and were soon inside the USAF controlled Da Nang airfield.

Several of the USAF units had recently departed as part of the US drawdown so there was plenty of billeting space to be had for the asking. I'm not saying the USAF had it plush but it was certainly a step or two up from our accommodations at Hue/Phu Bi.

While everyone was settling in I made contact with LTC J. who at the time was the overall leader of the SF MTT efforts in the aftermath of the Easter Offensive. He linked me up with the ARVN unit my MTT was to assist. Within a few days we were off and running.

My job as the MTT leader was part manager and part social / political. Green Berets are noted for their ability to interact with indigenous people but those of us who have done it for very long will tell you it does not come without hiccups, speed bumps and often total roadblocks. I spent a lot of time meeting with ARVN leaders, listening to their concerns and needs.

Most of these ARVN units had taken heavy casualties and were now resting and retrofitting. I explained what our MTT could do to better prepare them before they were moved back on line where enemy contact was almost certain.

Once we were in agreement there was still the matter of scheduling and resources. The NCO's conducted the training – my job was managing the hiccups and finding a way around the speed bumps and roadblocks.

Late one morning one of the NCO's and I were traversing the perimeter of the Da Nang airfield in our borrowed ¾ ton truck to deliver a much needed training aid. We were on the long side of the airstrip road as it turned sharply around the end. There was a fire truck ahead of us going at a high rate of speed in the same direction. To our astonishment the fire truck did not slow at the turn and did a slow motion double roll right before our eyes.

By the time we slowed and pulled up to the crash site the fire truck had stopped bottom side up with tires still spinning. Smoke was coming from what had recently been the engine block. The driver and his assistant could be seen stuffed inside the crumpled cab of the truck.

I ran to the wreck while shouting to the NCO, whose name after nearly fifty years I have forgotten, to flag someone down and send them for help. We didn't have a radio and of course this was eons before cell phones. Even if we had either we wouldn't have known who to call – my how times have changed.

As I squeezed under the wreck, fuel trickled out of the ruptured fuel tank and soaked my shirt and trousers. I remember thinking "Lord I hope that is diesel and not gasoline". My NCO had seen the same thing and shouted "Captain, get the hell out of there. That thing is about to blow".

Well, by that time I was committed so proceeded to pull and drag two badly injured Vietnamese Air Force firemen from the wreckage. The Lord must have heard me because the truck was fueled with diesel and did not blow.

We stayed around until an ambulance came for the injured and a wrecker to upright the truck. We then drove to our billets for a shower, change of clothes and a much needed beer. We were late delivering the training aid but had an excuse and good story to tell.

Young and dumb and living the adventure of our lives.

Chapter 20

Kids Love to Have Their Picture Taken

Pull a camera out when there are kids around and you end up drawing a crowd. I know some folks are thinking "how many fledgling VC in this picture". I may have been naive but I never thought that.

This photo is a young version of me, aka Captain K. in 1968. I was assigned as the Team Leader of A-415 (Tuyen Nhon) which was near the top of IV Corps just a little south of Saigon. The little fellow in striped shirt loved me and wanted to be picked up every time I saw him. The girl was the daughter of one of our interpreters. They all lived in the CIDG dependent village at the end of the airstrip.

This photo was used in a previous story but is worthy of repeating here. This little boy was the son of one of our camp workers. Our senior medic Perry Browning made arrangements for him and his mother to go to the Philippines where the harelip was corrected. It made a very favorable impression with the local population.

We had an airstrip right outside the front gate of our camp at Tuyen Nhon (A-415). The runway was covered with PSP (pierced or perforated steel planking). The PSP overlapped or hooked together to form a barrier to help distribute the weight of the aircraft.

One time a C-123 came in on a resupply run and swung too wide while turning at the end of the runway. This resulted in the front wheel ending up in the sand/mud. No amount of revving the engines could get it back on the runway. The crew ended up as our guests for the evening. They flew in some special gear the following day to extract them.

All the commotion attracted a big crowd from the nearby CIDG village. I grabbed my camera and lined up these young ladies for a picture.

Photo of one of our interpreters with his daughter and many of her friends.

Little sister / big sister / mother / close relative – I don't know. They smiled so I took their picture.

Smiles

And more smiles

This photo was taken during my last tour while I was leading the Armor MTT up near Hue / Phu Bai during the 1972 Easter Offensive. These folks were refugees who had recently been forced from their homes when the NVA pushed across the DMZ. Not many smiles here.

My little buddy again

How can you not have a soft spot in your heart for these kids?

Over the years I have often wondered what happened to them. Did they live a good life? Did any of them make it to the United States after the fall of Vietnam in 1975 or in subsequent years? How many of them are still alive?

So many unanswered questions. I know they touched my life and I am better for it.

Chapter 21

I Got Sick – Really Sick!

While we are all shut down due to the Covid-19 pandemic this might be a good opportunity for me to tell you about the time in Vietnam when I got sick – really sick.

First of all let me say I do not have a Purple Heart. I was there in the thick and thin during my first tour (68-69), not so much during the next time around and my extension until we declared "Peace with dishonor" (71-73). I am proud to say "I zigged when I was supposed to zig and zagged when I was supposed to zag".

My hat is off to those with Purple Heart's that are backed up with medical evacuation from place of injury and time spent in a hospital.

If you went back to duty the same day, ala John Kerry of the Swift Boat fame or LTC Viderman of the recent impeachment fiasco, don't ask me to look impressed. Being treated for scrapes and bruises by the unit medic and sent back to duty was not the criteria we followed for a Purple Heart in any of the units where I was assigned.

OK, now that I've got that out of the way let me tell you about my being sick. This took place about ½ way through my time as the S-3 (Operations Officer) of Phuoc Tuy Training Battalion (PTTB) where we were training Cambodians (FANK) and sending them back to their own country to join the fight.

My job was about ½ office type work (planning, lining up and allocating resources, issuing guidance and reporting results) and ½ out in the local and not so local area monitoring the actual training which was conducted by several SF training teams.

We had 3-4 Cambodian battalions cycling through at the same time. The only time my job got to the point of being what some might call "hairy" was at the end of each training cycle when the Cambodians went through a field exercise in an area which was supposed to be relatively clear of VC. As is always the case, the VC had a vote and sometimes did not know they were not allowed in the area.

When that happened my job entailed helping the Cambodians and their Green Beret trainers extract themselves with as few casualties as possible. I've written about accompanying medevacs to pick up the wounded & dead and night time resupply runs elsewhere in this series of short stories. Now let me tell you about my getting sick...............

For about a month I had experienced what could best be described as a bad case of the flu. Aches and pains, sweats and chills, headaches, etc. We had a doctor on site at Phuoc Tuy and he gave me antibiotics and whatever else he thought would cure it but it still hung on.

The doctor finally went to MAJ G. the battalion commander (before they upgraded all the battalion command slots to LTC) and said if we don't medevac CPT K. to the hospital in Saigon he might be in real trouble.

At the time I was the PTTB "fair haired boy" in MAJ G's eyes and he did not want to lose me. We all got our heads together and the doctor agreed that if he could have me report to the dispensary every afternoon for ten days that he would administer an hour of powerful antibiotic drugs intravenously. If that worked he would hold off on the medevac orders.

After about the third day of intravenous drugs I started to feel better and at the end of ten days was back to my normal self.

Just about that time there was a major shift in the FANK power structure with the battalion command slots being upgraded to LTC and FANK headquarters, located at Bien Hoa now commanded by a COL. My mentor MAJ G. was transferred to Bien Hoa.

About two months later the NVA pushed the ARVN off the DMZ and southward down Highway 1, past the city of Hue. FANK Training Command (FTC) pulled together a cadre of SF personnel to rush to the Hue/Phu Bai area to help reorganize and retrain the decimated ARVN troops and get them back into the fight.

My friend and mentor, MAJ G. who was now at FANK HQ in Bien Hoa tasked me to lead the Armor MTT. From that time forward until about 7 months later when we declared "Peace with dishonor" I was so busy that I don't recall if I was feeling poorly or not.

What I do remember is shortly after returning stateside and being assigned to the 82nd Airborne Division at Fort Bragg, I started to get terrible migraine headaches accompanied by nausea and diarrhea. I could tell when one was coming on because about a half hour prior my face would get all flushed and my vision blur.

I went to our battalion doctor who referred me to the post hospital where I had all sorts of tests to include brain scans but nothing definitive could be determined.

I gritted my teeth and did a successful stance as company commander in the 82nd. About a year later I was promoted and was off to Fort Leavenworth for the Command & General Staff College. My migraines went with me.

As luck would have it I was reassigned back to Fort Bragg, migraines and all. Not long after being reassigned to Fort Bragg, COL "Charging Charlie" Beckwith was forming up Delta Force.

I tried out and was doing fine until one morning before final selection my name was called out and I was ushered into COL Beckwith's office where he and his medical advisor were seated with my open medical file.

First thing out of "Charging Charlie's" mouth was "what are you going to do if one of these headaches comes on where you almost black out while on a mission?" I told him that I had learned to deal with them and would turn it over to my 2nd in command but he wasn't buying it. He concluded the interview with "one of the hardest things I have to do as a commander is telling volunteers that we can't use them."

And that is as close as I got to Delta Force. Probably just as well because I may have been one of those left to burn in the failed attempt in Iran to rescue the American embassy hostages two years later.

For the most part at that stage in my military career I was assigned to an office environment and whenever I felt a migraine or whatever was ailing me coming on I would place my phone on hold, close the office door and lie down on the floor for an hour or so.

I did catch a tour with the American Embassy in Cairo, Egypt where I spent a lot of time in the desert which seemed to mitigate the severity of the headaches.

I came back to Fort Bragg for assignment to the USASWC managing MTT's throughout the Mideast and North Africa. That job required a lot of travel which suited me fine. The problem was still there but manageable with high octane ibuprofen. For the most part they consisted of a constant low grade headache with occasional flare-ups to full blown migraines.

Once again I did all the medical diagnostic tests but nothing conclusive was ever determined. One doctor even put me down as a "mental case" – when I saw that I almost proved him right by going over his head and insisted on additional tests which also came back inconclusive. Everyone agreed it was more than just my imagination and the "mental case" notation was removed from my file.

I retired in 1990. I could have stayed longer but got orders to the Pentagon which did not fit with my long term plans so I retired.

I thought I was in pretty good shape other than wearing hearing aids and the headaches but the doctor who did my retirement physical said "you're going to have some problems down the road." Boy was he right!

So, what caused the headaches? I don't recall any blows to the head. I was near a lot of explosions but don't recall any concussions. Was it malaria or Agent Orange that required the 10 days of intravenous antibiotics? Nobody knows.

I still get the headaches but have learned to live with them. VA rated them at 30%. When you combine that with all my other ratings I top out at 160% - like that retirement doctor said a few problems showed up down the road. Maybe I should have kept that "mental case" notation in my file. I could have probably hit the 200% mark.

Chapter 22

We Won the Battles but Lost the War

Up to this point all my short stories have been factual with real people and real events that I played a part. This one is a combination of fact and opinion – that opinion is mine alone and may differ from that of others.

I arrived in Vietnam in 1968 while we were still building up the USA role in the war. Lyndon Johnson was president. He was still floundering around for a strategy. By then our KIA numbered about 25,000 which means we still had close to 35,000 KIA to go.

Most of the USA action was taking place in regions north of Saigon, i.e. III, II, and I Corps. The region south of Saigon, designated as IV Corps was also a hotbed of VC activity but was mostly left to the ARVN to handle.

I was assigned to a Special Forces (Green Beret) unit in a province at the top of IV Corps. We were strung out in a series of SF camps along the Vietnamese / Cambodian border. Each camp consisted of 3-4 companies of

Civilian Irregular Defense Group (CIDG) soldiers.

The CIDG program was similar to our National Guard i.e. soldiers from the local area – membership was also a good way to avoid being drafted into the regular ARVN and being sent to fight far from home.

During the 1968-69 timeframe, Cambodia was "off limits" to the USA war effort. Of course the enemy took advantage this and used Cambodia as a safe haven or sanctuary. Our mission was to collect intelligence, monitor infiltration routes and set up ambushes to limit incursions from across the border.

It was very frustrating trying to stop the flow of enemy personnel and arms along that very long and lightly defended border. It was sort of like fighting with one hand tied behind our back – we'd shut down one infiltration route and another would spring up a short distance away.

I rotated out in 1969 therefore was not there when everything changed in the spring of 1970. Recently elected President Nixon ordered a limited incursion into Cambodia to wipe out the enemy camps. For the remainder of 1970 from all accounts we really "took it to the enemy" and just about had the war won.

While we were winning the war on the ground we were losing it back home. The war had never been popular with the home front and that unpopularity intensified when Nixon ordered the invasion of Cambodia. The USA KIA numbers climbed past 40,000.

Bowing to public pressure Nixon announced a new strategy. We would turn over the fighting to the South Vietnamese in what became known as "Vietnamization" of the war.

The emphasis was now on equipping, training and advising regular Vietnamese Army (ARVN) units to the extent that they could take the lead in all the fighting.

Unfortunately 5th Special Forces Group, who were the best USA soldiers trained for working with foreign troops had been deemed non-essential and sent home shortly after the infamous "Green Beret Affair".

Regular army officers and NCO's soon found themselves designated as trainers and advisors with the emphasis to certify Vietnamese unit's battle ready

ASAP so that USA units could be sent home.

It did not take the enemy long to realize they could just wait us out. They still applied pressure from time to time and inflicted 10,000 more USA KIA but it was obvious we were leaving. Among the USA troops no one wanted to be the last KIA.

When I rotated home in 1969 my assignment was to the Armor Officers Advanced Course. The next course of instruction didn't start until later that year. I was temporarily assigned as an instructor to a unit teaching Laotian officers advanced leadership skills. I really enjoyed that and put my Special Forces training to good use.

When the Armor Advanced Course started about half of us were Vietnam vets. It was then that I realized not everyone wanted to serve in Vietnam. The other half of my class were senior Captains or junior Majors who had somehow avoided that fate. They had recently been assigned to Germany or Korea and were all angling to go back to a similar assignment.

I was a high school dropout with a GED and close to 60 hours of night school college credits so jumped at the opportunity to finish my degree at the University of Tampa once my military school was finished. I took an accelerated course load at UT and graduated in 1971.

By this time the USA involvement in the Vietnam War was winding down but it was understood that "payback" for attending college on the "government's dime" was orders back to Vietnam. A lot of my fellow "degree completion" contemporaries were able to put that off by dragging out their studies in hopes the drawdown of troops would not make assignment back to Vietnam a near certainty. Not me, I got a taste of it during my first tour and found it to my liking.

One of my fellow UT students had been the aide to a newly minted Brigadier General who had oversight of the few Special Forces who remained in country once the 5th SFG(A) cased their colors and left. Through that connection I was able to receive orders directly to the USAV unit training Cambodians known as the FANK Training Command (FTC). I arrived back in Vietnam midsummer 1971.

In my view we had the war all but won by the time I returned in 1971. At the very least we had it won in the areas I became very familiar with.

I was assigned to the Cambodian training camp of Phuoc Tuy which was located on the Long Hai Peninsula about a 30 minute drive to the former USA in-country R&R resort of Vung Tau, 2 hours to the FTC headquarters in Bien Hoa and 2 ½ hours to Saigon.

The drive to Bien Hoa ran right past some of the rubber plantations which had been the scene of fierce fighting only a year or so prior. When I first arrived at Phuoc Tuy if you wanted to drive to any of the aforementioned locations you thought nothing of going with a single jeep – it was just a pleasant drive.

If you wanted to impress the few remaining Americans at any of those locations you cocked your Green Beret low over your right eye, put on your sun glasses and strapped a 45 pistol low to your hip. If you wanted to give the impression of a seasoned war fighter you strapped on your web gear and carried your M-16.

That all changed in early 1972 when the so called "peace talks" started to stall.

It was still obvious that the USA was "hell bent" to get out of Vietnam. The politicians and the military higher-up were saying the South Vietnamese were ready to go it on their own. The folks on the ground knew better – the war was going downhill right before our eyes.

That pleasant drive to Bien Hoa or Saigon soon required a convoy with gun vehicles to the front and rear. The Cambodian training camps at Phuoc Tuy and our sister camp Long Hai were also coming under frequent attack which was unheard off when I first arrived.

In the late spring of 1972 the NVA made a major push across the DMZ in what was later called the Easter Offensive. Myself and several others were pulled from our Cambodian training duties and formed up into Mobile Training Teams (MTT) and rushed to the Hue / Phu Bia area to help the ARVN reorganize and push back to the DMZ. My contribution to that effort is the subject of a previous short story titled "Armor MTT to Hue / Phu Bia".

After standing down from MTT duty I was reassigned as the Operations Officer (S-3) for FTC. We didn't have an officer filling the S-2 slot, so with the aid of a very competent NCO, I filled that role as well.

My new job made me a part of a fact finding team that flew to Phnom Penh, Cambodia to assess the Cambodian government's ability to conduct their own training. It was our conclusion they were not ready but that did not go over very well with the military staff at the embassy. It appeared that decisions had already been made and the Cambodian military would soon be on their own.

When we closed out the Cambodian training program at Phuoc Tuy and our sister camp about 3 miles up the road at Long Hai we organized a heavily armed convoy with helicopter gunships overhead to get them all out. By the end of 1972 the road to Vung Tau and the Long Hai Peninsula was closed all together.

The FTC mission changed from training Cambodians to providing MTT's to ARVN units which had previously been certified as combat ready by USA "Vietnamization" advisors eager to work themselves out of a job.

We ran these MTT's with a small residual force of in-country Special Forces personnel augmented with teams from 1st SFG(A), TDY from Okinawa. Again this is my opinion – The "Vietnamization" program should have been using SF personnel all along. Special Forces (Green Berets) are trained in the skills necessary to successfully interact with foreign nationals.

What we were doing with the MTT's was too little, too late. While we were working diligently to shore up the ARVN, the so called "Peace Talks" were going on and the USA footprint in Vietnam was being rapidly reduced.

Toward the end it was a numbers game, i.e. we had to be down to a certain number of personnel at the end of each month. To get around that we would send MTT"s from Okinawa back home on the 29th and recall them on the 1st.

Every time the peace talks would stall the enemy let us know they were still there with a rocket attack on the Bien

Hoa Airfield. FANK Training Command was located along one edge of the airfield. One attack dropped a rocket in our motor pool and another just outside our command section building. The rocket which burst just outside the command section sent shrapnel through the wall and made a direct hit on the FTC commander's high back office chair. If the attack had come during the day instead of in the wee hours of the morning FTC would have been looking for a new commander.

The Paris Peace Accords aka "Peace with ~~Honor~~ Dishonor" were signed on January 27th 1973. In accordance with this agreement the United States would end it's involvement with Vietnamese affairs. Within 60 days all USA military personnel were to be withdrawn. Interestingly, it did not say anything about the withdrawal of North Vietnamese forces from the south.

FTC immediately recalled all of it's MTT's. The TDY teams from Okinawa were sent home and the few teams that were assigned directly to FTC were the first ones programmed for assignments stateside.

The staff of FTC headquarters busied itself with preparing to "abandon ship". The first consideration was what to do with all the accumulated paper work and reports. We'd seen this coming so many of the after action reports were already in draft form.

There was also an awful lot of stuff that just plain needed to be destroyed – no shredders back in those days so it all went into an almost continuously lit burn barrel.

The two biggest dilemmas or jobs were the responsibility of the S-1 (Personnel) and the S-4 (Supply).

The S-1 had to work the personnel system to obtain immediate stateside assignments for about 40 senior NCO's and officers. I initially received orders to Ft Hood, TX but those were later amended to Ft Bragg, NC.

The S-1 was also responsible for the smooth termination of 75-100 civilian indigenous personnel - boy that was a mess. My heart goes out to those folks, many of whom had worked faithfully with us for many years. We just plain abandoned them.

The S-4 had to turn over all property to include buildings, vehicles, armament, and all gear other than personal clothing to a representative of the ARVN. There was no problem with the buildings – what was there is what you got.

The problem was with the rest of it. Being Special Forces we had lived up to our reputation and accumulated lots of stuff off the books. During the 2 years of the drawdown, every time an American unit was leaving we begged, borrowed and sometimes just plain appropriated things we thought we could use.

We had 4 jeeps on the books but in reality just about everyone had their own jeep. I had my own jeep and enough armament to hold off a small army. In addition to my issued M-16, I'd accumulated an AR-15, 45 pistol, 38 revolver and neat little 25 automatic. My guess is the ARVN were happy to look the other way at the lack of paperwork. A lot of it likely made it's way to the black-market.

About 35 days after the signing of the Paris Peace Accords I was driven to Saigon by an ARVN driver, to what remained of the USARV G-1 Section, where I checked in. The ARVN driver departed with my "off the books" jeep to never be seen again.

The USARV G-1 assigned me to a billet in a nearby hotel and told me to come back once a day to scan a bulletin board where a roster or manifest would be posted with names of those departing on hastily arranged flights for that particular day. 3-4 days later my name came up.

I reported to Tan Son Nhut Airbase, just outside of Saigon, where I, along with about 100 others, was placed on a bus and driven to a stairway leading up to a chartered passenger airplane. There was a blue helmeted Canadian and Polish officer with clipboard checking our names as we walked up the stairway. It seems the United Nations was checking to make sure the United States did not cheat and leave anyone behind. I remember distinctly that I was number 529 which means there were 528 others behind me. It took the better part of another month for us all to leave.

I don't think they had anyone at the DMZ to check off the NVA as they marched their troops back into North Vietnam.

I know a lot of folks say we gave it our best shot and maybe we did. I sure wish it had turned out different – but it didn't. Some will also say the South Vietnamese lost the war – but to those I say "maybe, but at least they held out 2 years longer that we did".

Who knows what would have happened if we had not abandoned them?

Chapter 23

Random Thoughts

I heard the rat-tat-tat of a machine gun and saw the dirt kicking up around my feet and thought, "Damn, that guy is aiming at me"

Ho Chi Minh had a saying "If not in my lifetime, maybe my children's lifetime. If not in their lifetime maybe in my grandchildren's life time" or words to that effect - In other words he was in it for the long haul. The American public did not have that long term perspective.

Looking back, we did a lot of stupid things. But we were young, invincible and thought if anything bad happened it would happen to the other guy.

I was in Special Forces and we were pretty well isolated from the goings on with the rest of the US military. The only time I saw a drug problem was when we had a US Navy "Swift Boat" unit move in to work with us.

No family support systems back in those days. When you shipped out to Vietnam your wife and kids went back home and waited for your return. Nobody called to check on them - they were on their own. It was hard on families - it still is.

Vietnam was a beautiful country and the people in the south were very friendly and industrious. They wanted what most freedom loving people want for their family and their country. They did not want centralized planning or autocratic government, but that is what they ended up with when we pulled the support away from them.

When we went from low key counter-insurgency and nation building to large scale direct action search and destroy missions we started losing the war. We won the battles but we caused so many civilian displacements and casualties that we drove a lot of the people over to the other side.

When we returned to the USA they used to time our arrival at Travis or McCord AFB for after midnight to help keep encounters between protestors and the military to a minimum. We changed to civilian clothes for the next leg of our journey home.

Despite all the problems associated with the war, I'm glad I did it. I'm proud to call myself a Vietnam Vet.

Miscellaneous Pictures

Most people who spent time in Vietnam will recognize this place.

HQ, 5th Special Forces Group (Airborne) Na Trang, Vietnam

Captain K. 1ˢᵗ time on patrol. Note the cleaning rod readily available to clear malfunctions. A short time later they replaced the bolts which helped.

Captain K. near the end of his tour. A seasoned warrior by this time.

Twelve "little people" lined up and waiting for a Huey ride back to camp.

Chow time. We fed the CIDG well. In the field they were issued dehydrated rice and shrimp – just add water and a little hot sauce. Very good!

Happy CIDG – They conducted a successful ambush last evening – 6 VC KIA which was my Christmas present to the B team commander who wondered if we ever got outside the wire.

All smiles – everyone shows up on payday

Local transportation.

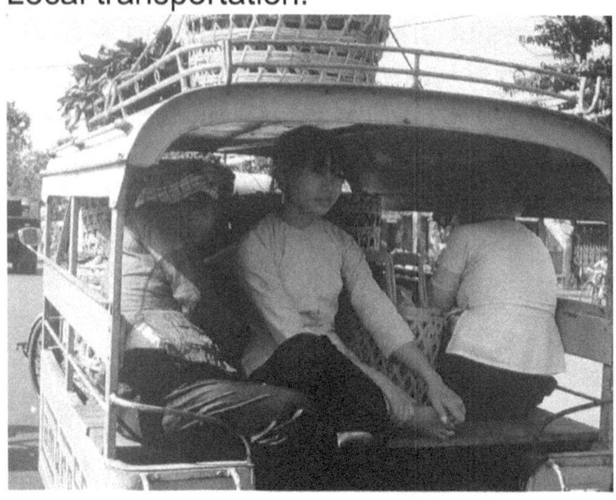

Manpowed Moped – These guys had powerful leg muscles.

This monument was just outside the gate at Tan Son Nhut Airbase for all to see. The inscription said "Thank you American Fighting Men – We Will Never Forget Your Sacrifice"

Imperial Palace, Saigon, RVN. In 1975 NVA tanks rolled right over the exterior fencing.

Special Acknowledgements

A big THANK YOU to Terry McIntosh whom was one of my communications specialists at A-414 (Thanh Tri) for encouraging me to write this book. Terry is an author and film producer who has documented his experiences during that era.

Terry's own autobiography "The Youngest Green Beret" about his time in Vietnam is available on Amazon.

E-book:
https://www.amazon.com/dp/B07N8GKKWT
Paperback:
https://www.amazon.com/dp/173151784X

His video "Double Agent Down – The Green Beret Affair" is now available for viewing on U-tube
https://youtu.be/1gE3g-4K-ng.

A special thank you to my lovely wife Anita Kittredge who spent many hours proof reading so this kid who quit school in the 10th grade would not be a major embarrassment.

www.ingramcontent.com/pod-product-compliance
Lightning Source LLC
Chambersburg PA
CBHW060533160726
47991CB00001B/309